THE CRAFT OF

Florentine Embroidery

BARBARA SNOOK

Charles Scribner's Sons, New York

Printed in the United States of America
Library of Congress Catalog Card Number 75-165164
SBN 684-12502-1

Acknowledgments

My grateful thanks to Mrs. Joan Toggitt who suggested the need
for this book; to Mr. Hilary Gardner, Librarian of the Embroiderers'
Guild, for all his help in the initial stages of research; to my students
for their practical assistance, and to Miss Elinor Parker and Mrs.
Margareta F. Lyons for their interest and care in producing this book.

$\mathcal{T}$he term Florentine is used here to cover varieties of Florentine stitch and Hungarian point. These two stitches are distinct but the type of design on which they are used overlaps to such an extent that the two cannot be studied separately. Florentine stitch can be variously stepped, generally forming a zigzag line.

Flame or lightning patterns, developments of the zigzag, are formed with either Florentine or Hungarian point.

In certain elaborate floral designs Hungarian point is the dominant stitch forming a zigzag background as well as pattern on the motifs.

Groundings for use on canvas, mainly of 19th century origin, are based on Florentine stitch, Hungarian stitch and Hungarian point, and have an important part to play in present day canvas embroidery.

There is a tendency to think that certain stitches should always be used alone, Tent stitch (petit point) being an outstanding example of this belief, yet comparatively few pieces of historical embroidery have been worked entirely in one stitch. In Florentine embroidery not only are other stitches included, but very often part of the design is worked with stitches at right angles to the rest.

FLORENTINE EMBROIDERY

A most versatile type of embroidery, Florentine, if accepted in its widest sense, offers far greater scope for use today than if we restrict the connotation to the variety known as 'flame' which is indeed the least adaptable of all its forms. However, in its adaptation to present day use all Florentine methods call for considerable restraint in both choice of colour and scale of design.

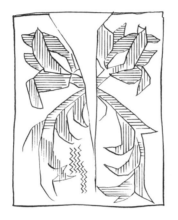

Fragment worked in floss silk on linen canvas
Probably Italian
Tulip-type flowers shaded pink to cream
Leaves shaded green—yellow-green
Background, an acid yellow worked in Byzantine stitch
   in a much coarser thread than the floral motif
Size 7½″ x 9″
Diagram to show direction of Florentine stitch 4.2 step

1. CANVAS

Single thread canvas used for Florentine stitch and Hungarian point embroidery is obtainable in various widths and threads to one inch, from 14 threads, which is fairly coarse, 16, 18, 20, 23, 24, to 28 which is very fine.

The number of threads to one inch in other fabrics which may be used is given here for comparison, and is only an approximate guide because texture and firmness of weave also affect the choice of material on which to work, for example, a 28 thread canvas appears very fine and does in fact permit more detailed work than a 30 thread even-weave material.

	Threads to 1″	*Manufacturer*
"Lauder" linen gauze	33	Old Glamis
"Willow" cross stitch material	30	Dryad
Even-weave linen	25, 28, 29	Glenshee (Richmond Bros.)
Norland openweave linen	22	Dryad
Coarse Willow	18	Dryad
Linen, various	13–19	Old Glamis
Embroidery fabrics, various	17–19	Glenshee

5

2. SUITABLE FABRICS OTHER THAN CANVAS

When Florentine stitch in any of its numerous forms is to be used as an open design, in lines or a spot arrangement, and not as on canvas, a close filling, the material on which the embroidery is worked shares in the colour scheme. Almost any even-weave material can be used and other fairly loosely woven fabrics where it is possible to count the threads.

Coarse Willow cross stitch material in natural, and Willow embroidery fabric in several colours, are much softer to handle than fine canvas. Glenshee mercerised cottons are of similar weight and Glenshee even-weave linens with a bright sheen, available in several widths and colours, are excellent to use.

Hardanger cloth with threads woven in pairs, is obtainable in white, natural and several colours; it has only one slight disadvantage in that warp and weft threads are not exactly of the same thickness so that a design becomes a little longer one way than the other. If the embroidery is worked in one direction no problem arises.

Norland openweave linen and Lauder linen gauze generally used for drawn fabric work may at first sight appear uncompromising material, but it proves a very pleasant ground on which to work in wool, stranded cotton and Sylko perlé (pearl cotton). Threads withdrawn from the material itself can be used for drawing the threads together if pulled (drawn) fabric work is introduced for further variety. This type of linen does not lose its shape unless carelessly handled; however, only a reasonably experienced needlewoman will attempt experimental work of this nature.

Fine flannel and dress weight woollens can be used only if the threads in the weave are distinguishable. Some Scandinavian furnishing fabrics, especially those made in Finland, are almost like woollen gauze, and evoke new ideas in the field of Florentine embroidery.

3. THREADS

WOOL   Appleton's Crewel wool
Penelope Crewel wool, W. Briggs
Various 2 and 3 ply knitting wools and Angora wool
"Anchor" Tapisserie wool
Beehive Tapestry wool
Appleton's Tapestry wool
Kelim wool, similar in weight to double knitting

COTTON   Clark's Stranded cotton
Clark's Coton à Broder
Clark's "Anchor" Soft
Dewhurst's Sylko Perlé or Pearl Cotton No. 5
D. M. C. Stranded cotton
D. M. C. Sylko Perlé or Pearl Cotton No. 5

SILK   Unfortunately nothing has yet replaced Filoselle which is no longer manufactured. Floss silk is obtainable, but is so difficult to handle on any but the finest canvas that it may be disregarded by all but the most experienced needlewomen.

4. NEEDLES

FOR EMBROIDERY
  Tapestry   blunt tip, large eye, 24 (small)–13 (very large)
            24 is suitable for all fine canvases
            22 can be used on an 18 thread to 1″ canvas

FOR MAKING UP
  Sharps   No. 8 is recommended for general use.

5. RELATIONSHIP OF THREAD TO FABRIC

Canvas mesh and thread thickness must be considered simultaneously. If possible, experiments should be made on several different fabrics before work is begun. Threads of the same thickness need not be used throughout a design, but any change in thickness should be deliberate and purposeful, contributing to the texture of the work. While it is good that everyone should experiment, one rule must be observed . . . when canvas is used the mesh must be completely covered. Different makes of wool vary in their spinning; some are quite even and can be used one piece at a time; others equally good, may be uneven and should therefore be used double so that slight variations in thickness counteract one another.

Stranded cottons may be used 3, 4, or 6 strands at a time according to need. Sylko Perlé (Pearl cotton) can be used only if it fills the canvas mesh; on even-weave linen it is a successful contrast to stranded cotton.

Three ply knitting wool tends to work up thicker than crewel wool and if used on the same piece of embroidery, gives a different height and texture.

On fabrics other than canvas, which by their nature contribute to the finished work, all threads to be used must be tested for their appearance. They should lie smoothly together to give an even surface.

6. COLOUR CHOICE; CARE OF THREADS

Threads are available in a wide colour range. Their combined total surpasses the needs of any embroideress today. In the "Boat" panel 45 shades were used and in the "Owl" 13 shades, but in more orthodox designs 14 could easily be enough, allowing for 7 shades each of two colours.

Colours can, unwisely, be chosen from a shade card, which, while indicating the range, shows too small a piece to be of much use and the colours cannot be tested against each other. Even a selection of skeins in the hand can be deceptive; in the example (p. 61) pink and grey looked much more attractive in the skein; when actually worked, their tone contrast proved to be too great.

Colours must, without exception, be chosen in daylight; any form of artificial lighting plays strange tricks with both colour and tone. However, since much work will be done in artificial light, it is essential to see that colours are securely numbered . . . number tags too easily come adrift. A container made from a long band of linen or improvised from a strip of sheet, with a wide piece of tape stapled at 1″ intervals along the centre, makes a satisfactory cover for threads. If these are arranged in shade order with each number written on the tape, confusion can be avoided. Any odd usable lengths of thread should, when cut from the work, be slipped at once through their appropriate compartment. When using a finely graded colour range, it is quite impossible to distinguish single threads by any light other than daylight.

786 | 785 | 784 | 783 | 506 | 505 | 504

partly used lengths

9

Colour schemes must always be considered with their setting and use clearly in mind. Within the available wide range of threads deep rich colour schemes are as easily created as those which are very light and delicate, or softly subdued. Threads nowadays are normally fast colour. If only one thread in a subtle colour scheme fades to a different tone, many hours' work are wasted. Colour schemes in historical examples are not always easy to assess because fading has taken place at different rates. Generally blues, greens and yellows of the 17th and 18th century have faded very little whereas purple and in particular, the pink shades, have often changed to very lovely mushroom tones unobtainable at that time. While contemporary trends will always affect our choice of a colour scheme, a worthwhile piece of embroidery is not finished in a day, and the hours of work expended will only be justified if what we have made will endure for many years and has a lasting quality unaffected by the tides of fashion.

7. DESIGN

A glance through Part II will give some idea of the range of patterns in Florentine embroidery design. This is by no means an exhaustive collection. The slightest variations lead to other patterns; in fact, possibilities are almost infinite.

The patterns, however, do seem to fall into certain groups, some of which are more suited than others to present day use. On the whole the smaller, more compact, groundings are easier to live with than the huge repeats of the 17th and 18th centuries.

PLACING THE DESIGN ON THE FABRIC

If a traditional design is chosen, the position of the first line on the fabric can be worked out by counting; thereafter, row succeeds row and the sole guide needed is a small pencil sketch with thread colours recorded on it. This sounds simple enough, but it may in fact take a little time to establish the exact position of motifs in a piece of work like the hexagonal cushion on p. 67.

Even with the help of graph paper, variations in design are not always easy to work out correctly.

Florentine stitch has, in the past, frequently been used with other stitches. The modern approach to this aspect of the work can be found in Part III and Part IV.

8. TEXTURE

The regular 4.2 step gives a monotonous texture and interest depends entirely on the colour arrangement and on the introduction of different threads. Historically, this fact was appreciated. In the familiar carnation pattern, silk used in contrast to wool, either in part of the background or part of the motif, or in outlining the main shape, does much to alleviate the stitch's monotony. The chief 'break through' in the combination of texture and colour came with the joint evolution of Hungarian ground and the 'flame' design, and the appearance of the subsidiary pattern which surely was at first accidental.

The importance of texture in design should not be underrated. There are no hard and fast rules to follow. In the napkin ring (p. 64) a smooth texture contrasts with the homespun cloth. The hexagonal cushion could have been worked with certain rows in a thicker or shiny thread. Such decisions are a matter of personal choice, but if in doubt, it is wiser not to strive too hard, too obviously, for the unusual effect. (See also Part IV, Modern Design.)

11

9. FRAMES

Florentine stitch, being worked on the straight thread, does not need to be mounted in a frame, the use of which tends to immobilise the embroideress. Though essential for some kinds of canvas work in which certain stitches pull the canvas diagonally, a frame is all too often used for some imaginary prestige value. Work, carefully folded or better still, rolled, keeps in shape for as long as any piece of embroidery should take to do. Stretching over damp blotting paper (See p. 16) or pressing face downwards into a soft blanket brings the work to pristine freshness.

No frame has been used for any modern specimens in this book.

10. WORKING METHOD

Florentine patterns are based on an upright stitch; the line pattern depends on the length of stitch, length of step and the number of stitches in each step.

A stitch passing over 8 threads of canvas can be counted a long stitch; too many such, unless the thread is well chosen, will make a flimsy piece of work. Steps over 4, back 2, and 6.3 or 6.1 are more practical. Alternatively too short a stitch with very thick thread makes a hard lumpy fabric and too thick a thread also suffers during its passage to and fro, being frayed and roughened, which again results in untidy, uneven embroidery.

A Victorian woman, writing in 1842,* tells us "The needleful of wool should be short, both on account of soiling and impoverish-

* *Handbook of Needlework* by Miss Lambert published by John Murray 1842.

ing as it passes through the canvas, and a very small portion only should be passed through the eye of the needle. Finishing off on the same spot should always be avoided". For comfort wool should be

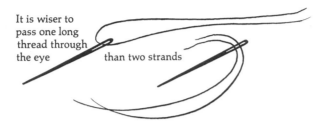

It is wiser to pass one long thread through the eye than two strands

about 16″ long and it is wise to move its position in the eye of the needle two or three times to avoid weakening the wool in one place. Doubled wool (above) should be cut to allow a 16″ working length. The loop in the eye may wear slightly but this will be cut away in any case when the thread is finished off. Two threads through the eye pass less easily through the mesh. There is no place for securing the beginning of the first thread until this piece has been used; therefore, to prevent the first stitches from slipping, the thread should begin with a knot at a point about 2″ from the first stitch. Immediately this first thread has been used and its final end darned into the back of the work, the knot must be snipped off and the end darned in. As work progresses there is more room for securing the ends which must not accumulate in one place as this causes an uneven surface.

Some Florentine patterns such as those in B group have much more wool on the back than do others, for example those in E group. This should be considered when making a design; a very thick stitch will produce a too bulky small article whereas the same stitch may be advantageous on a stool top where additional padding cannot come amiss.

The need to balance thickness of thread with mesh of canvas cannot be emphasised too often. If the canvas is not entirely covered, 13

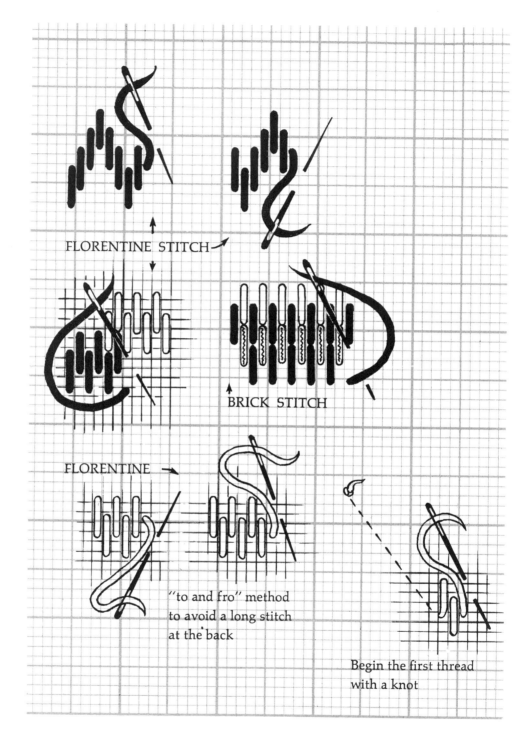

FLORENTINE STITCH

BRICK STITCH

FLORENTINE

"to and fro" method
to avoid a long stitch
at the back

Begin the first thread
with a knot

flecks of light mesh showing through between the stitches disturb the design, prove that the thread is not thick enough and consequently that the work will not wear well. Canvas and wool together have great endurance, proved by some 17th and 18th century work in use within living memory, and while we may not expect our work to last 200 or 300 years, we should do our best to make it technically sound.

11. GENERAL PRACTICAL NOTES

1. On canvas protect the edges by oversewing or binding, to prevent fraying.

2. Do not cut curves or diagonal edges until work is finished; a rectangular piece of canvas keeps in shape.

3. Allow a generous margin beyond the design.

4. On materials other than canvas a guide line tacked to indicate the final shape may be helpful in determining where to finish or adjust a row of stitches.

5. Lay threads side by side to make certain of their colour relationship to one another; write down their order as a precaution against mistakes which easily occur in artificial light.

6. Keep a needle threaded with each colour.

7. Use short lengths of stranded cotton and Sylko perlé to avoid losing their gloss, and short lengths of wool to avoid weakening the fibres by too frequent passage through the canvas.

8. When making up work, always oversew canvas from the right side, between every embroidery stitch, with cotton which sinks invisibly into the embroidery.

12. STRETCHING FINISHED CANVAS WORK

A completed piece of embroidery on canvas will need stretching to its original size, in spite of the fact that it may not have taken up noticeably while it has been worked. Stretching should be done by placing several sheets of clean blotting paper on a clean board, important because stain can percolate up through the fabric. The embroidery is thumb-tacked to the board, right side up, beginning in one corner, pulling very hard along one edge while keeping it parallel with the edge of the board; the adjacent edge is pinned next, then the two other sides. If the whole process is done patiently, working round several times, pulling outwards a little more each time, the pins will not bounce out too often, a tantalising occurrence. This task is hard on the fingers and there is no easy way out. To ensure that the work is pulled true, with right-angled corners, the edge of the fabric should be measured from the edge of the board with a gauge. When all is well, water is carefully trickled on to the blotting paper, *behind the embroidery,* until saturation point is reached. The front of the embroidery itself must not get wet. About 24 hours should elapse before the work, quite dry, and beautifully freshened, is released.

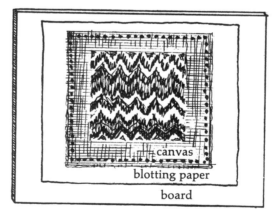

16

13. FRESHENING EMBROIDERY WHICH HAS NOT BEEN WORKED ON CANVAS

Florentine embroidery which has not been worked on canvas should be placed face downwards on a blanket and gently pressed from the wrong side, easing the fabric outwards from the center. This method was used for the beaded vanity bag (p. 83) and the apron (p. 84), both worked on "Willow" cross stitch material, and for the owl (p. 91) worked on loosely woven linen.

14. MAKING UP FINISHED WORK

Surprising though it may seem, a good embroideress is not necessarily a good needlewoman when it comes to making up her embroidery. Excellent work can easily be ruined and made to appear clumsily amateurish if careful sewing technique is not completely followed through to the end. To many of us this final stage is tedious. Attaching other material to canvas must be done by hand, sewing between every thread of the mesh, with small straight oversewing stitches, always working from the right side because the work is too thick to be turned inside out.

In Part IV details are given of the different stages involved in making up several of the examples created for this book.

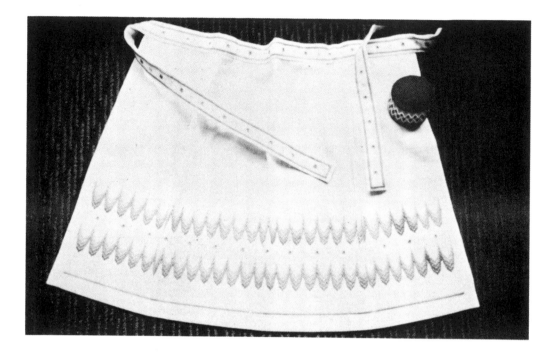

A child's apron (directions on page 84) and a detail of the border

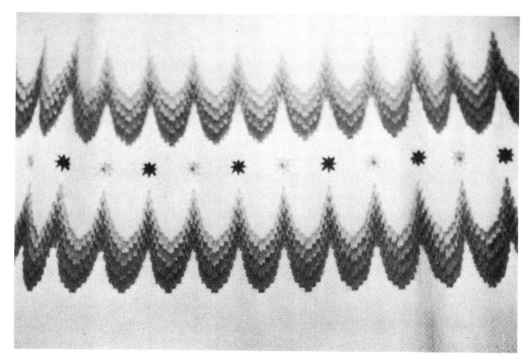

INTRODUCTION

Although these patterns fall into fairly clearly defined groups a slight alteration in either length of stitch or number of stitches in each step can change the pattern from one type to another. Some of the smaller designs, particularly those which do not have a continuous line running through them, could equally well be considered as "groundings" a term for which it is difficult to find a true definition. (See page 45)

A1. UNBROKEN LINES

Same number of stitches in each step
Same length step
Same length stitch

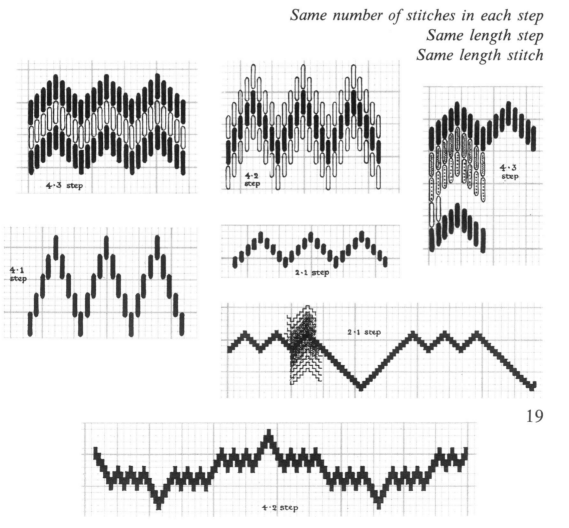

19

FLORENTINE EMBROIDERY

A1. UNBROKEN LINES

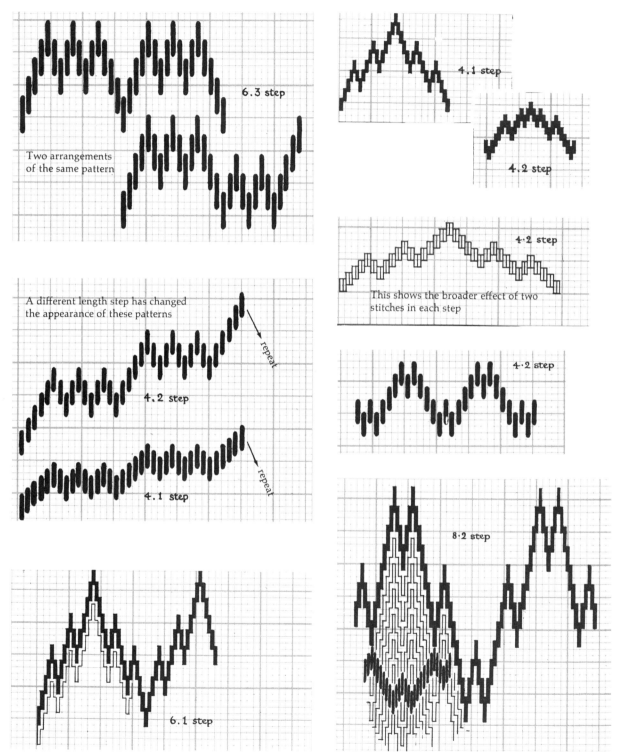

6.3 step

Two arrangements of the same pattern

4.1 step

4.2 step

4.2 step

This shows the broader effect of two stitches in each step

A different length step has changed the appearance of these patterns

4.2 step

4.2 step

repeat

4.1 step

repeat

6.1 step

8.2 step

A1. UNBROKEN LINES

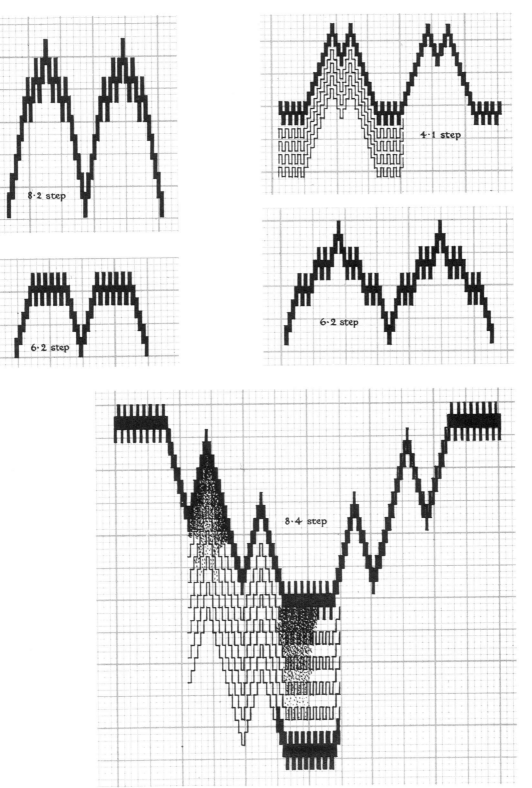

8·2 step

6·2 step

4·1 step

6·2 step

8·4 step

A2. PARTLY BROKEN LINES

Same number of stitches in each step
Same length step
Same length stitch

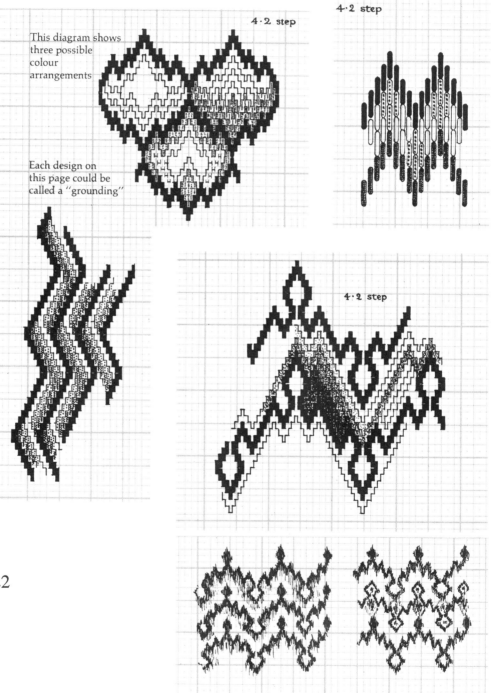

This diagram shows three possible colour arrangements

4·2 step

4·2 step

Each design on this page could be called a "grounding"

4·2 step

A2. PARTLY BROKEN LINES

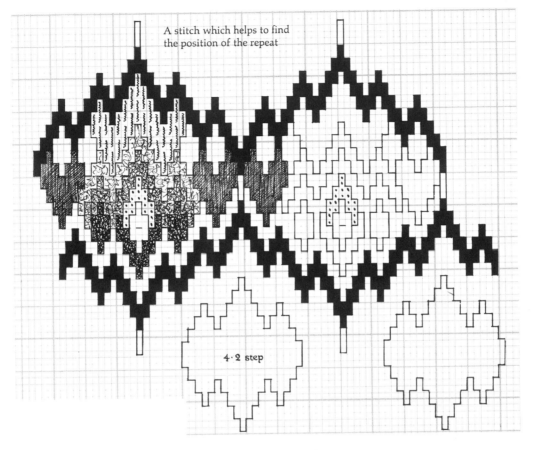

A stitch which helps to find
the position of the repeat

4·2 step

Sketch to show the
effect of a tone change
on alternate bands

A2. PARTLY BROKEN LINES

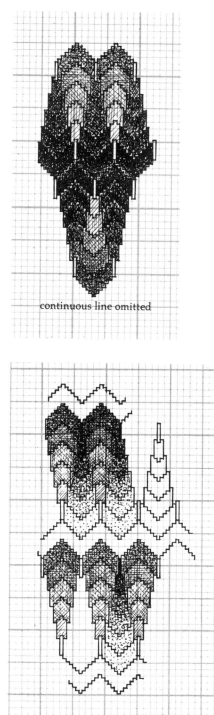

continuous line omitted

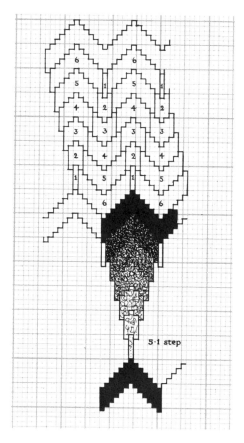

5·1 step

A3. BROKEN LINES

Same number of stitches in each step
Same length step
Same length stitch
These are also Groundings G2 type

"BASKET WEAVE"
PATTERNS

Each block represents
2 stitches

All 4·2 step

B1. UNBROKEN LINES

Variable number of stitches in each step
Same length step
Same length stitch

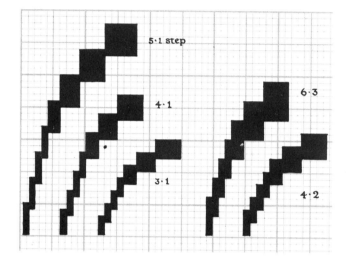

Group B patterns being akin to satin stitch, have much wool on the back. This should be taken into account when designing small articles. If the blocks of stitches are pulled too tightly, the mesh is exposed, a fact well known to the Victorians who exploited the horizontal stitch they darned in as a cover, sometimes only making matters worse by over-emphasising the line with too thick a thread or too strongly contrasting a colour.

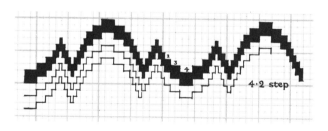

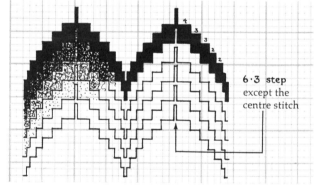

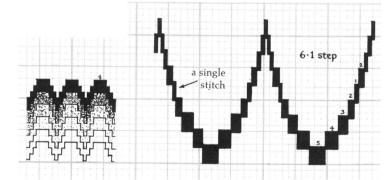

26

B1. UNBROKEN LINES

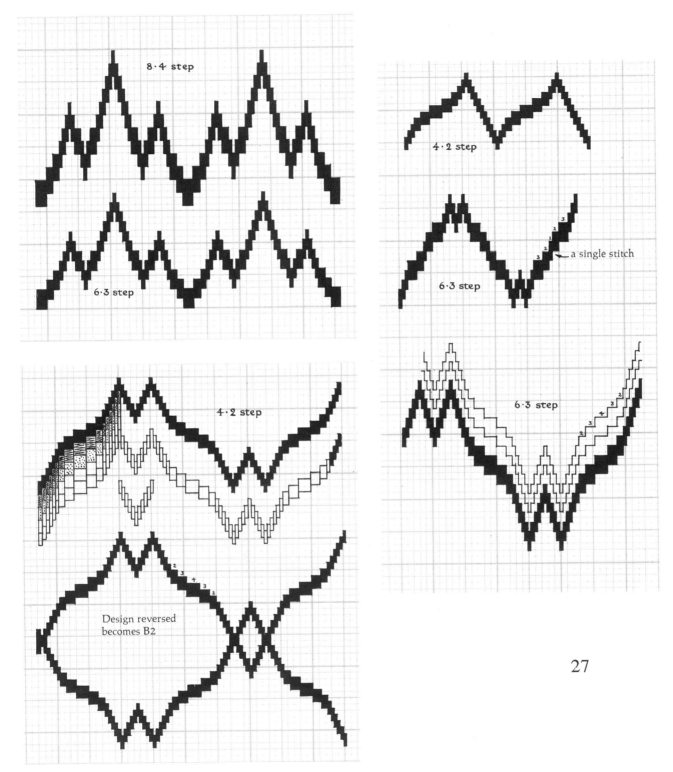

8·4 step

6·3 step

4·2 step

6·3 step

a single stitch

4·2 step

6·3 step

Design reversed
becomes B2

27

B1. UNBROKEN LINES

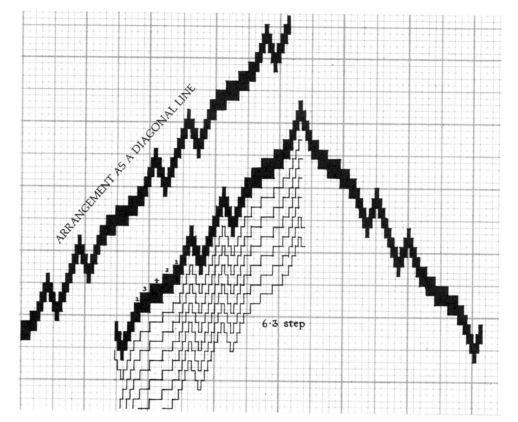

ARRANGEMENT AS A DIAGONAL LINE

6·3 step

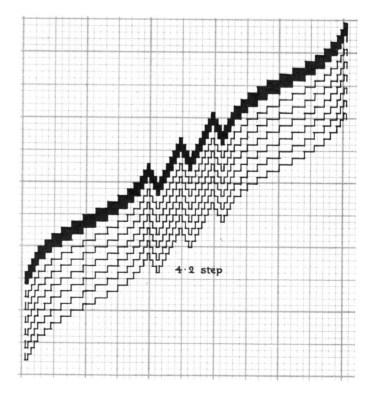

4·2 step

28

B1. UNBROKEN LINES

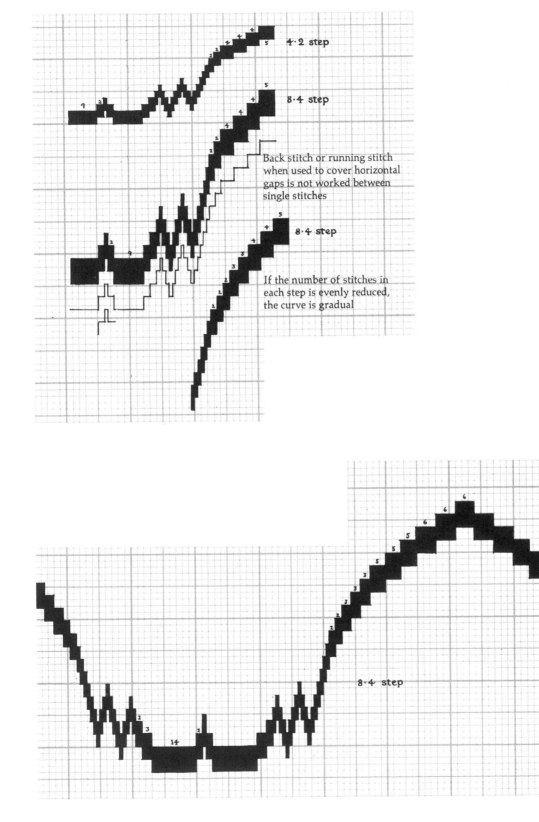

4·2 step

8·4 step

Back stitch or running stitch when used to cover horizontal gaps is not worked between single stitches

8·4 step

If the number of stitches in each step is evenly reduced, the curve is gradual

8·4 step

B1. UNBROKEN LINES

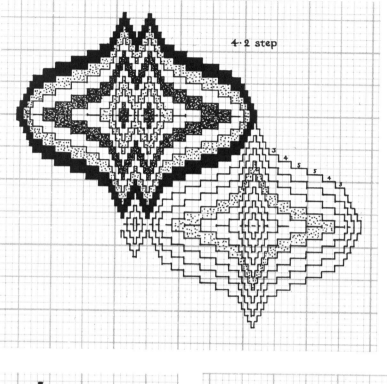

4·2 step

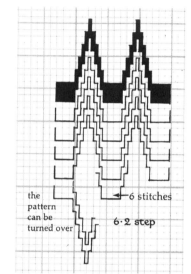

the pattern can be turned over

6 stitches

6·2 step

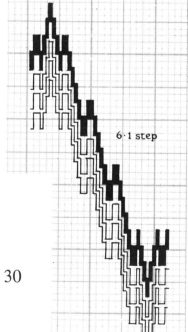

6·1 step

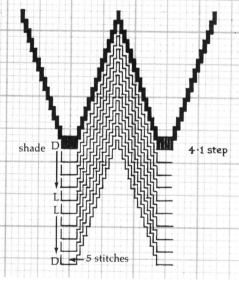

shade D

L
L

DL ← 5 stitches

4·1 step

30

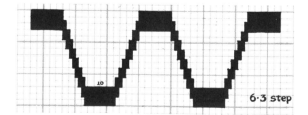

6·3 step

DIAGRAMS OF PATTERNS

B1. UNBROKEN LINES

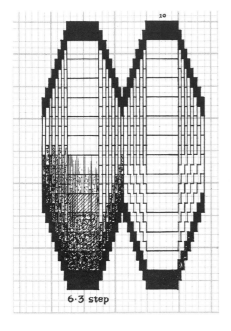

6·3 step

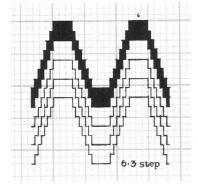

6·3 step

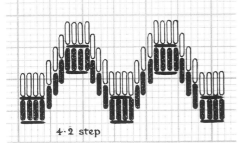

4·2 step

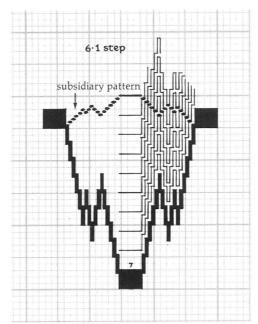

6·1 step

subsidiary pattern

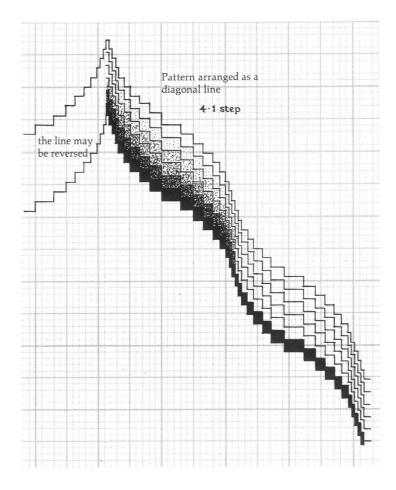

Pattern arranged as a
diagonal line

4·1 step

the line may
be reversed

B2. USUALLY *ONE* CONTINUOUS LINE, THE OTHER LINES BROKEN

Variable number of stitches in each step
Same length step
Same length stitch, except where an occasional small stitch is needed to make the pattern fit
All the smaller patterns could be called Groundings

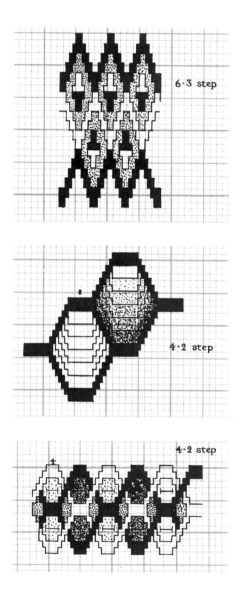

6·3 step

4·2 step

4·2 step

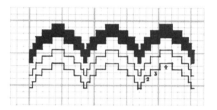

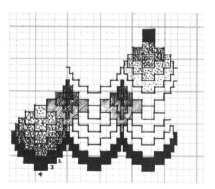

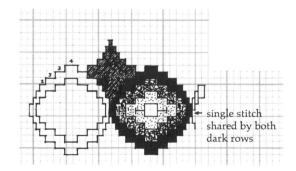

← single stitch shared by both dark rows

B2. USUALLY *ONE* CONTINUOUS LINE, THE OTHER LINES BROKEN

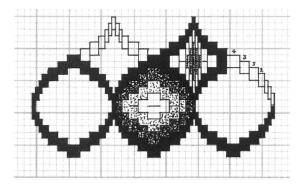

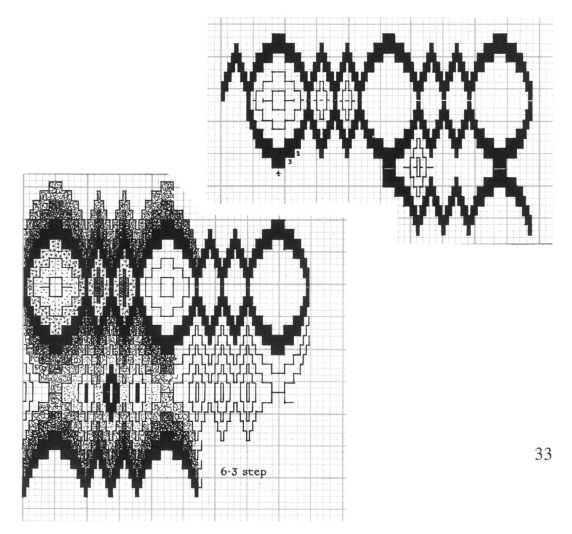

33

B2. USUALLY *ONE* CONTINUOUS LINE, THE OTHER LINES BROKEN

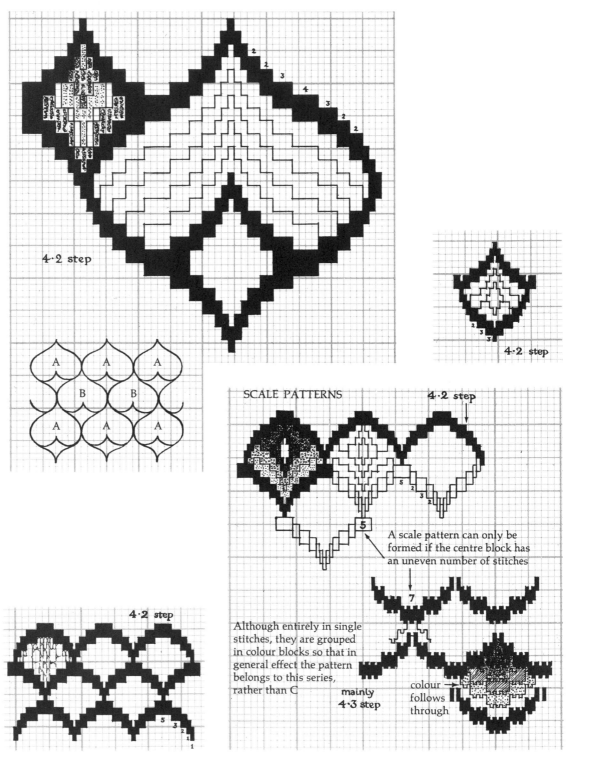

4·2 step

A A A
B B
A A A

4·2 step

SCALE PATTERNS   4·2 step

A scale pattern can only be
formed if the centre block has
an uneven number of stitches

Although entirely in single
stitches, they are grouped
in colour blocks so that in
general effect the pattern
belongs to this series,
rather than C

colour
follows
through

mainly
4·3 step

4·2 step

B2. USUALLY *ONE* CONTINUOUS LINE, THE OTHER LINES BROKEN

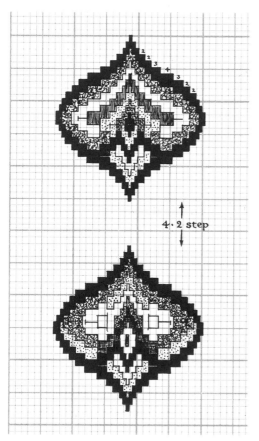

4·2 step

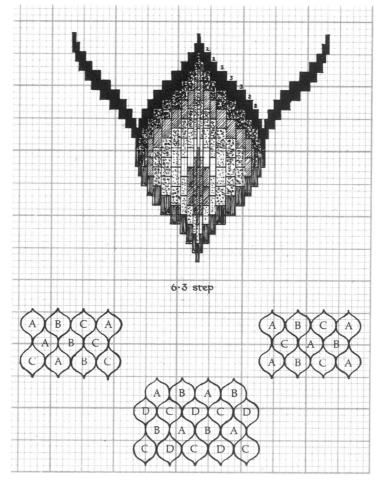

6·3 step

C.

Single stitches
Same length stitches
Different length step

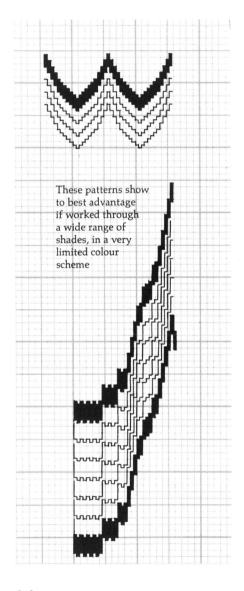

These patterns show
to best advantage
if worked through
a wide range of
shades, in a very
limited colour
scheme

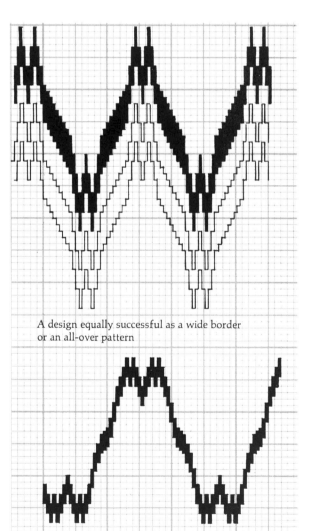

A design equally successful as a wide border
or an all-over pattern

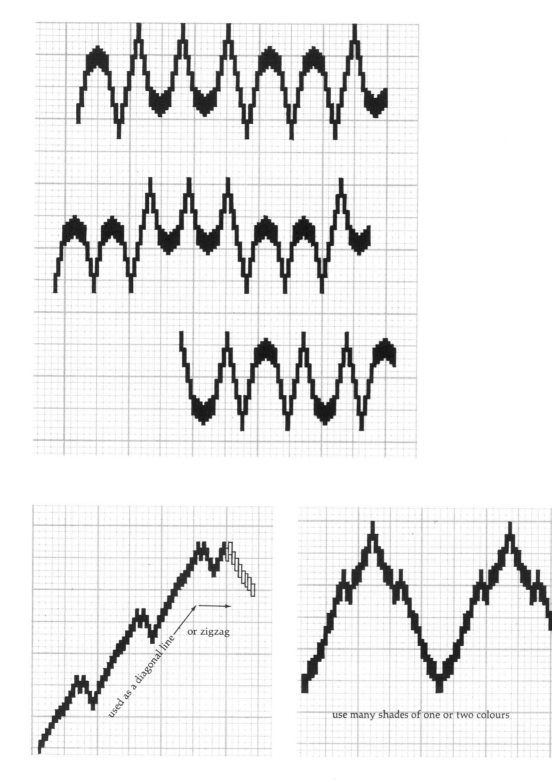

used as a diagonal line — or zigzag

use many shades of one or two colours

C.

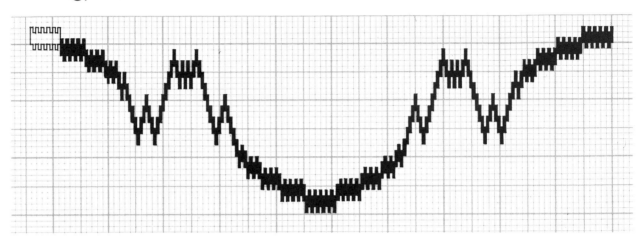

D.

Same number of stitches in each step
Varied length of step
Varied length stitch

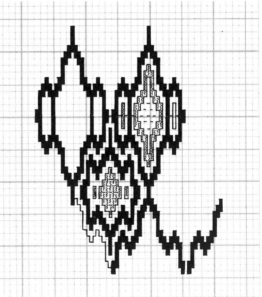

E1. HUNGARIAN POINT

One large stitch
Two small stitches

The term Hungarian Point is used to describe a particular method in Florentine embroidery. It is worked in rows of single stitches, in steps of 1 long, 2 short; 2 long 2 short; 1 long and 3 or more short. The patterns are exceedingly confusing to copy and to work, even when it is realised that a "1 long 2 short" line will repeat on the third line and a "1 long 3 short" pattern will repeat on the fourth line. In *drafting* it helps to remember that if a vertical line is followed, one long stitch comes in line with two or three short as the case may be. (below)

In historical examples the repeat is usually completely hidden by a wide range of tints spreading over many rows before these in turn repeat themselves.

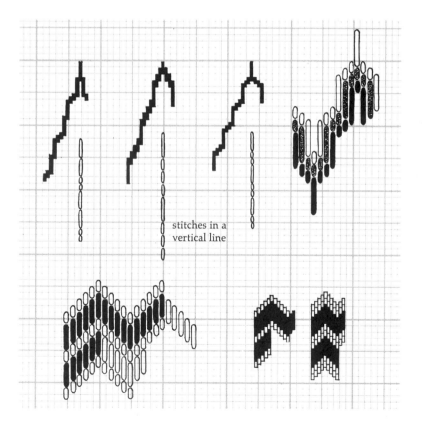

stitches in a
vertical line

E1. HUNGARIAN POINT

Another complication is the presence of a subsidiary pattern which appears somewhat mysteriously as the result of the shape of the main repeat line. This gives an interesting additional texture and further enriches already elaborate work.

Hungarian Point, to be seen at its best, must cover a very large area. Of all the Florentine embroideries this striking pattern is least suited to the present day home.

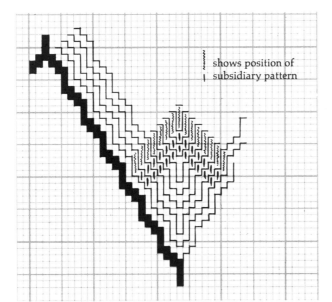

shows position of subsidiary pattern

40

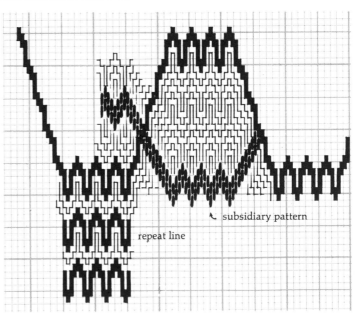

subsidiary pattern

repeat line

E2.

Two large stitches
Two small stitches

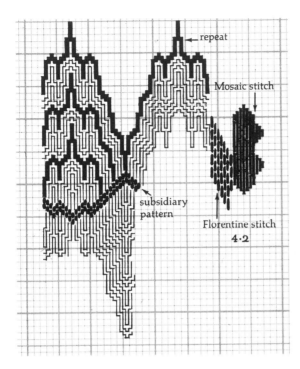

On the original the colours were used without regular repetition, eleven rows shaded blue from dark to light, three rows brown and gold, two white, three pink, seven fawn, brown, gold, brown, two white and eight shades of green. This resulted in the absolute disappearance of the true repeat in the pattern and it was not discovered until the cartoon was drawn. The subsidiary zigzag merely gave varied texture. The source of this design, an unfinished panel worked in filoselle on a soft canvas, with narrow dividing borders of mosaic stitch, is in all probability late 19th century work. Its purpose is unknown, but the softness of the cotton canvas suggests that it was intended as a hanging.

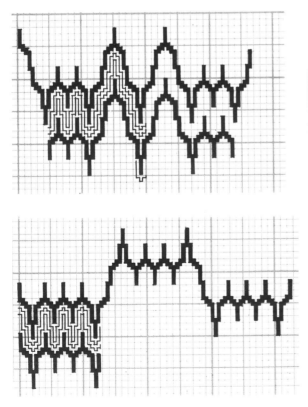

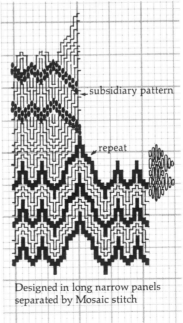

Designed in long narrow panels separated by Mosaic stitch

41

E2.

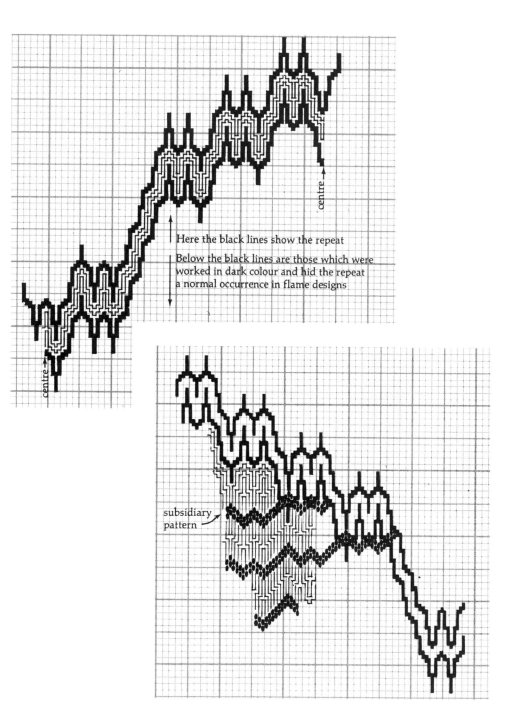

Here the black lines show the repeat

Below the black lines are those which were
worked in dark colour and hid the repeat
a normal occurrence in flame designs

centre

centre

subsidiary
pattern

E3.

One large stitch
Two small stitches

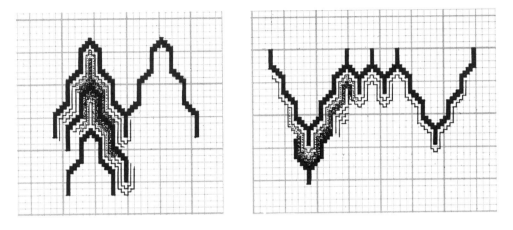

E4.

Other variations

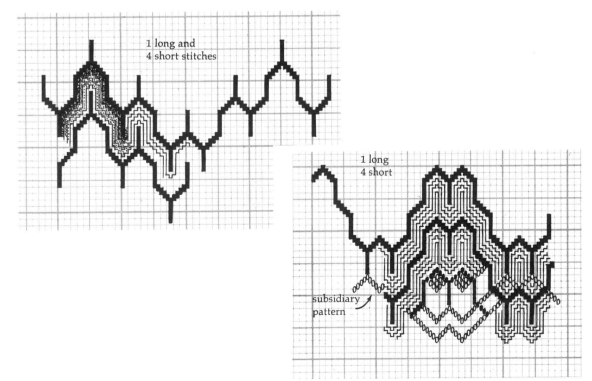

E4.

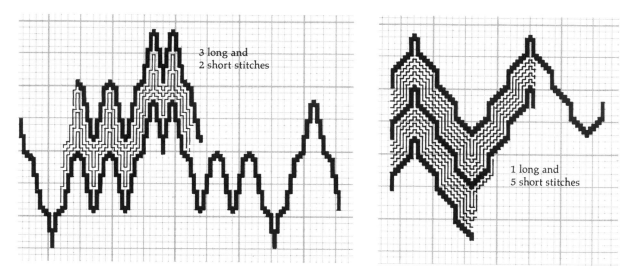

ANALYSIS CHART

DIAGRAM TO SHOW THE MAIN VARIATIONS IN THE STEP ARRANGEMENT FOUND IN FLORENTINE PATTERNS					
NUMBER OF STITCHES IN EACH STEP		LENGTH OF STITCH IN EACH STEP		LENGTH OF STEP IN EACH ROW	
CONSTANT	VARIABLE	CONSTANT	VARIABLE	CONSTANT	VARIABLE
A1		A1		A1	
A2		A2		A2	
A3		A3		A3	
	B1	B1		B1	
	B2	B2		B2	
C		C			C
D			D		D
based on Hungarian point { E1 E2 E3 E4				E1 E2 E3 E4	

GROUNDINGS

Grounding is the term in general use for a fairly small all-over pattern. We do not now simply mean background as does Miss Lambert, to quote again from her Victorian book, "It is curious that the grounding, one of the most particular parts of the work, should generally be deemed of such minor importance. Although a tedious and uninteresting process, yet when properly accomplished, it fully repays the trouble bestowed." No one involved in the intricacies of a Florentine grounding will find the occupation tedious. Since Florentine embroidery is normally concerned in covering a whole area, any distinction between what may be called the main field of design and a background pattern is purely arbitrary.

Many patterns found in groups A–E can also be considered groundings, particularly those which do not have continuous lines of colour running through them, but even this is no absolute criterion.

MAIN VARIATIONS IN THE STEP ARRANGEMENT IN GROUNDINGS

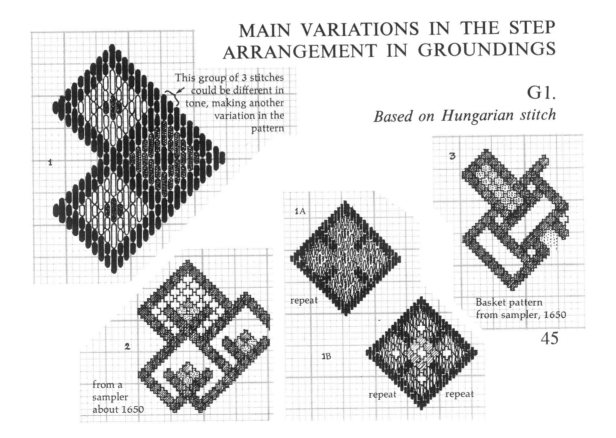

This group of 3 stitches could be different in tone, making another variation in the pattern

G1.

Based on Hungarian stitch

1A

repeat

1B

3

Basket pattern from sampler, 1650

2

from a sampler about 1650

repeat   repeat

45

FLORENTINE EMBROIDERY

G2.

Based on Florentine stitch,
4.2 step, with either one or
two stitches in a block

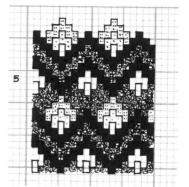

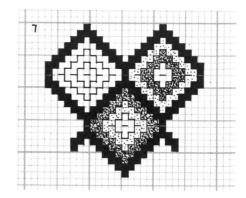

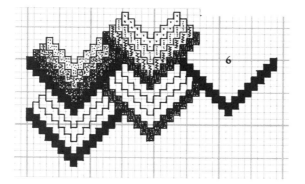

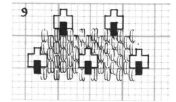

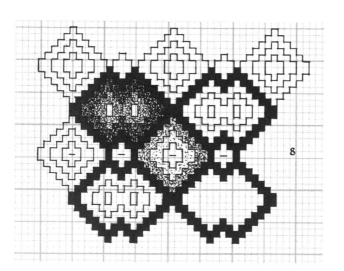

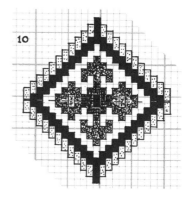

G2.

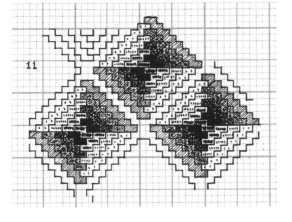

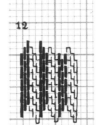

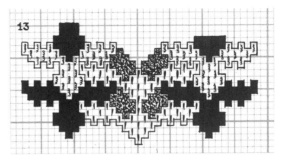

G3.

*Based on Florentine stitch,
regular step, evenly divided,
6.3, 2.1, etc.*

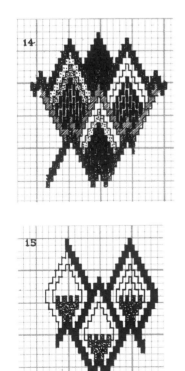

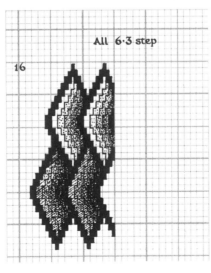

All 6·3 step

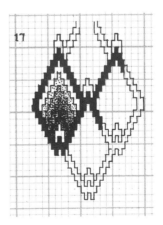

G3.

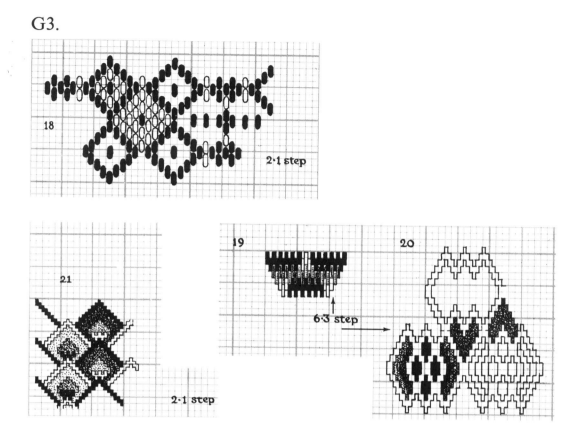

18

2·1 step

19

20

6·3 step

21

2·1 step

G4.

*Patterns with same length stitch
and variable number of
threads in each block*

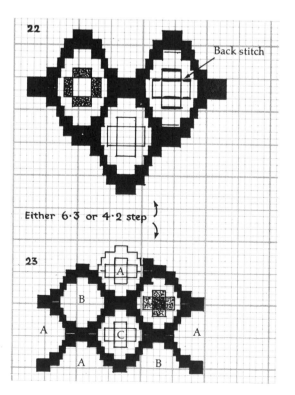

22

Back stitch

Either 6·3 or 4·2 step

23

A

B

A

C

A

B

colour
diagram

	B		A		B	
A		C		A		C
	A		B		A		B
	A		C		A		C
	A		B		A	

G5.

*Patterns with variable length stitch
and same number of
stitches in each block*

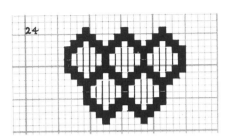

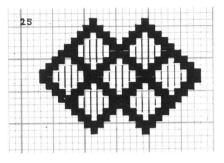

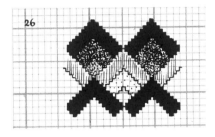

G6.

Other variations

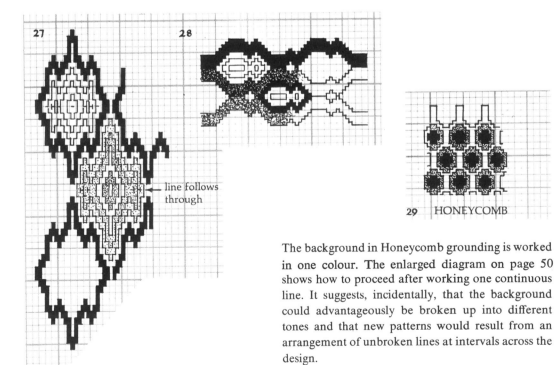

line follows
through

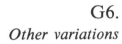

29 HONEYCOMB

The background in Honeycomb grounding is worked
in one colour. The enlarged diagram on page 50
shows how to proceed after working one continuous
line. It suggests, incidentally, that the background
could advantageously be broken up into different
tones and that new patterns would result from an
arrangement of unbroken lines at intervals across the
design.

G6.

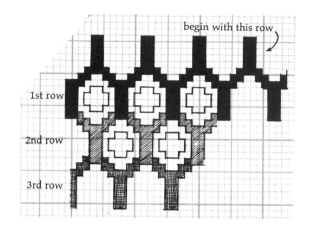

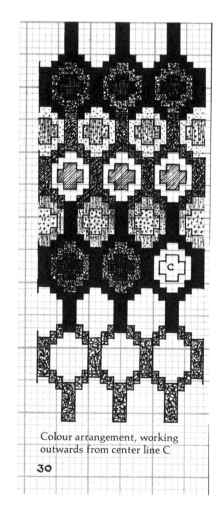

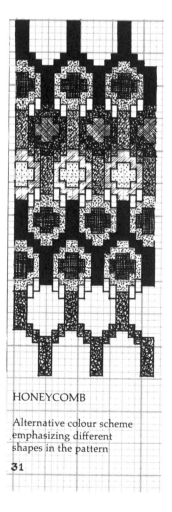

50

Colour arrangement, working
outwards from center line C

30

HONEYCOMB

Alternative colour scheme
emphasizing different
shapes in the pattern

31

G7.

*Patterns based, even remotely,
on Hungarian Point—E group*

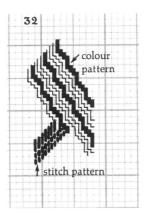

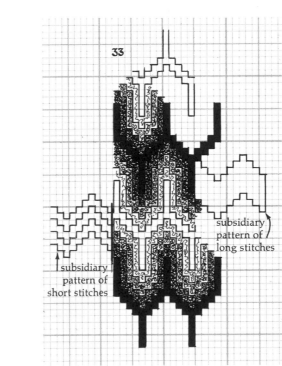

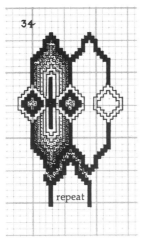

51

G7.

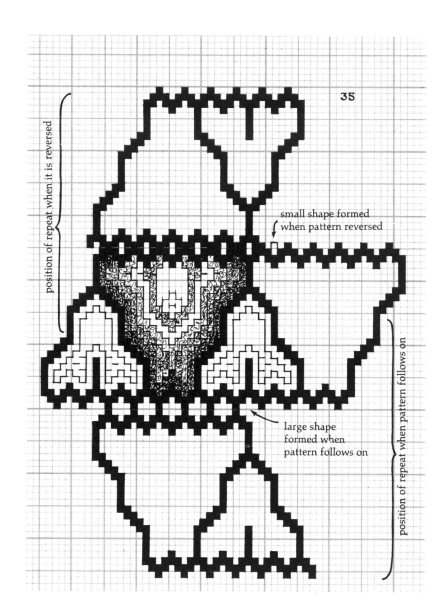

III • *Canvas Stitches to Use with Florentine Stitch and Hungarian Point*

USEFUL ADJOINING STITCHES

As we have already seen on historical examples, stitches other than Hungarian, Florentine and Hungarian point were used in Florentine embroidery; tent, Byzantine, mosaic stitch and French knots played their part in large Italian floral designs. We have noticed too, that where patterns have not worked out accurately, or where the stitchery has abruptly been turned at a right angle, stray stitches have quite simply been fitted in to fill the spaces. Nowadays we are more selfconscious about technique.

In a pictorial or abstract design with Florentine merely one amongst many other stitches, the transition from one stitch to another may affect the design itself. Only a few stitches link easily into Florentine and Hungarian stitches. Among canvas stitches worked on the straight thread the most suitable are:—

Byzantine, brick, upright Gobelin, straight Gobelin, Parisian, Hungarian ground and satin.

Other stitches worked over the diagonal thread, tent, cross, rice and eyelet, will not pull the canvas out of shape if used with discretion, that is, over very small areas or, in the case of eyelet, as an isolated stitch.

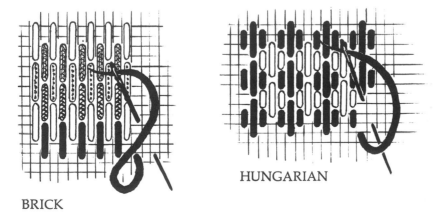

BRICK

HUNGARIAN

53

FLORENTINE EMBROIDERY

PARISIAN

UPRIGHT GOBELIN

HUNGARIAN GROUND

STRAIGHT GOBELIN

SATIN

CROSS STITCH

Each cross must be
made separately;
each stitch must cross
in the same direction

DIAMOND EYELET

EYE STITCH

Back stitch may
be needed
to cover canvas

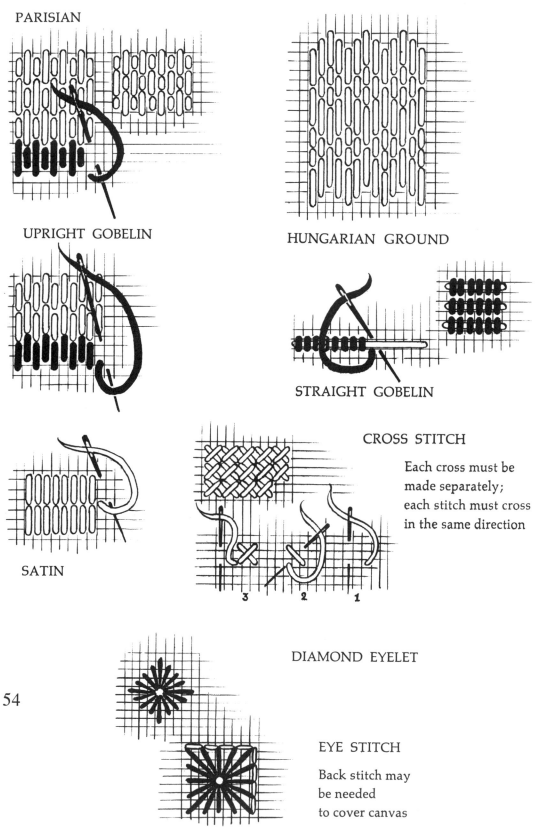

54

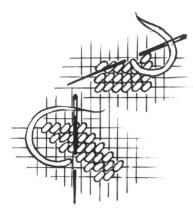

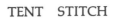

TENT   STITCH

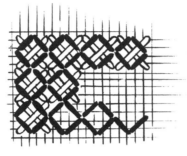

RICE STITCH

Work a ground of
cross stitch; tie
down each corner
by working two
horizontal rows of
diagonal stitches

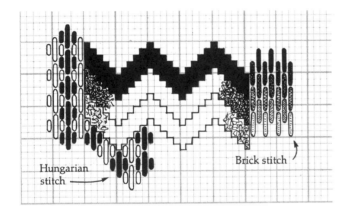

Hungarian
stitch

Brick stitch

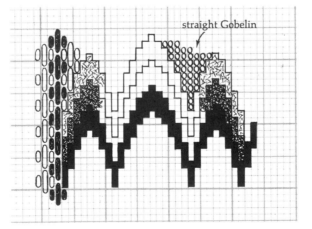

straight Gobelin

55

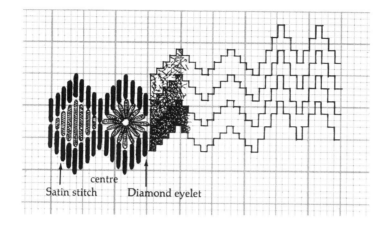

Satin stitch   centre   Diamond eyelet

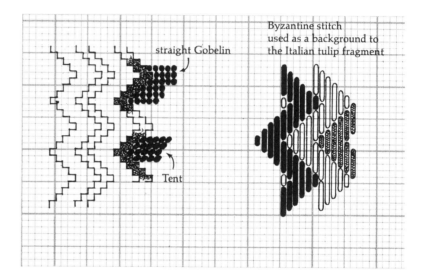

straight Gobelin

Tent

Byzantine stitch
used as a background to
the Italian tulip fragment

INTRODUCTION

The study of Florentine stitch and Hungarian point is but a fraction of the larger subject of canvas embroidery. The present day use of this can prove as stimulating to the designer as ever it did in the past. Certainly large hangings are unlikely to be needed, and even if they were, would require a corporate effort for their completion, but upholstery is within the scope of an individual embroideress, who can also make many small objects, each in a very short time. It is vitally important that the scale of pattern should be in accordance with the size of the article to be made; this, and the wise choice of colour and tone cannot be too often emphasised, and holds true for all canvas embroidery.

A design must always give the impression that it is an integral part of the object which has been made, that it has grown from the materials used and is not something afterwards applied. Today, with the widened range of suitable fabrics, many of them beautiful in both colour and texture, absolving us of the need to cover them completely, the designer can, within the limitations imposed by regular stitches, exploit these values and create unusual and individual work.

Two aspects of the use of Florentine stitch have not as yet been fully explored; the first, in pictorial design, and the second, in its relationship to materials other than canvas. Neither should be studied in isolation, and an attempt has been made in the succeeding pages to show the process by which designs may be evolved. The owl, 57

(p. 91) created from a design intended for canvas, developed instead on Norland open-weave linen, more freely than had been foreseen. The introduction of drawn fabric stitches in the background was not premeditated. On the body, patterns which began as Florentine stitch changed as work progressed. Such a liaison between mind, hand, fabric and thread can be likened to the unity which exists between an experienced horseman and his mount.

Designing comes easily to very few people; even the most fluent know that hiatus between one idea and the next, when it would seem that nothing new can ever be forthcoming. For most of us design involves considerable effort.

If we think of Florentine embroidery in terms of texture, as a varied means of covering a surface rather than as a series of zigzag lines, ideas may come more freely. With this in mind a study of modern French tapestries, particularly those of Jean Lurçat, can open up exciting vistas. His masterly treatment of feathers as a flat pattern, his angular shapes and unusual colour, are invigorating. From his work we learn that simplification does not mean monotony.

PRACTICAL NOTES

1. Ideas for design emanate from unexpected sources. In selection it must be remembered that shapes themselves should be simple, thus if inspiration comes from a prehistoric cave painting, that of a rhinoceros or a bison will adapt more successfully than a gazelle or giraffe because the former are essentially mass shapes while the latter are both linear.

2. Ideas for colour may be suggested by the leaves of a house plant, the subtle tones of driftwood, moss on a tree stump seen in the strange light of the rain forest, or in brilliant minerals with all their array of crystal formation.

3. Pattern ideas may come from rock strata in Yosemite, the convolutions of a shell, from the damp shore line on a rugged coast. To the alert eye all are potential design sources.

4. Most of the designs in Part IV are based on straightforward stitch arrangements shown in Part II. Sometimes a small piece of pattern has been taken from a grounding and turned into a spot motif which can easily be traced back to the original. Other work has taken advantage of the varied shapes and adaptability of Florentine lines, and the ease with which they can be shaded. Where a working cartoon is not given, reference is made to the pattern's source.

5. For the more ambitious needlewoman who wishes to create her own designs, students' sketches are included to show how the impetus of one idea leads to another and the process by which it goes forward to a finished piece of pictorial work.

6. Objects, not illustrated, which could be embroidered in Florentine stitch or Hungarian point:

  1. Toilet seat cover
  2. Bathroom mat on rug canvas, worked in rug wool
  3. Small rug on coarse canvas, 14 threads to 1″
  4. Screen
  5. Bedhead
  6. Upholstery for chairs or small seats
  7. Top and sides of a "pouffe"

PINCUSHION

MATERIAL	Single thread white canvas 23 threads to 1″ Felt for top and base
THREAD	Stranded cotton, blue, pink, white, yellow Sylko perlé No. 5 (Pearl cotton)
SIZE	1¼″ deep, 2¼″ diameter
TO MAKE UP	Join the side seam, sewing from the right side with matching cotton. Fold the edges over, creasing firmly and snipping them (diag. 1). Cut two felt circles without turnings to fit exactly at each end. Place one piece of felt in position and pin edge to edge (diag. 2). With cotton to match the felt, sew between every thread of canvas. Use short lengths of cotton and pull tightly. Sew on the other end in the same way, partially stuffing the pincushion when ⅔ sewn, adding fragments of stuffing as the gap closes.

DESIGN TYPE A2

snip edge of canvas

position of pins in felt

felt

1

2

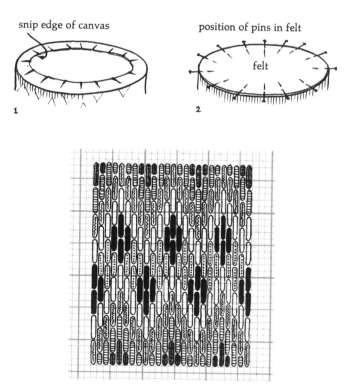

SCISSORS CASE

MATERIAL	Single thread white canvas 23 threads to 1″
	Buckram for stiffening. Silk lining
THREAD	Stranded cotton, shades of pink
SIZE	Back 4¾″ x 1¼″. Front 1¼″ x 3¼″
TO MAKE UP	Make the back separately with all turnings invisible. Line the embroidered front piece, also with hidden turnings; place both pieces together and oversew tightly from the outside.

DESIGN TYPE B1

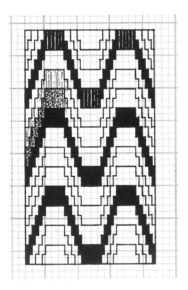

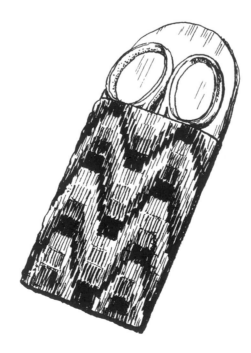

61

NEEDLECASE

MATERIAL	Glenshee Evenweave linen, 28 threads to 1″ Linen lining. Cardboard
THREAD	Stranded cotton
SIZE	Approximately 3″ x 4″. Let this depend on a convenient number of repeats in the design.
TO MAKE UP	Surround the design with a ¼″ band of tent stitch to make a good edge. Work reverse tent stitch down the spine of the book. Hem stitch and fringe several flannel pages or cut with pinking shears. Crease the linen lining straight by the thread; turn down the canvas; place wrong sides together and oversew the two long edges, working from the right side between every thread of the canvas. Sew the hemstitched pages to the spine, catching on to the canvas with invisible stitches. Slip the cardboard into place from each end and close the ends with oversewing.

DESIGN TYPE A3

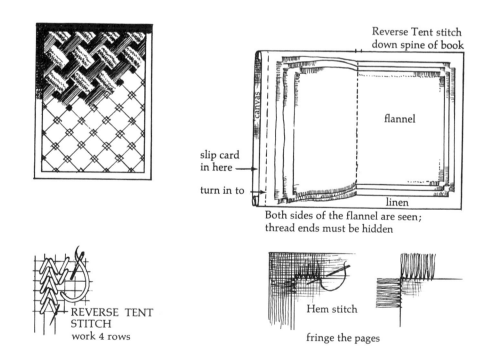

Reverse Tent stitch
down spine of book

canvas

flannel

slip card
in here →

turn in to

linen

Both sides of the flannel are seen;
thread ends must be hidden

REVERSE TENT
STITCH
work 4 rows

Hem stitch

fringe the pages

TELEPHONE BOOK OR
WRITING CASE COVER

MATERIAL   Single thread canvas, 23 threads to 1″ or Glenshee linen,
leaving part of the pattern unworked to incorporate the colour of the fabric in the design.

THREAD   Crewel wool or stranded cotton

It is advisable to have the work mounted professionally on a
leather case; therefore a margin of at least 1″ of unworked canvas
should be left beyond the design.

DESIGN TYPE D

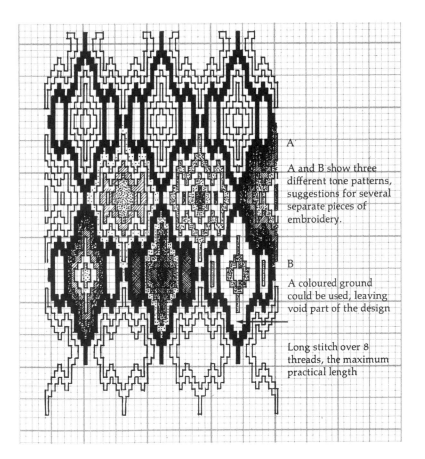

A

A and B show three
different tone patterns,
suggestions for several
separate pieces of
embroidery.

B

A coloured ground
could be used, leaving
void part of the design

Long stitch over 8
threads, the maximum
practical length

63

NAPKIN RING

MATERIAL	Single thread white canvas 23 threads to 1″
	Linen lining
THREAD	Stranded cotton
SIZE	2¼″ x 5¾″ circumference
TO MAKE UP	If the pattern at each end is so arranged that it matches perfectly the ring can be joined invisibly. Make the lining slightly smaller; open out the seams, place them face to face; turn in upper and lower edges; oversew the two pieces together, sewing between each thread of the canvas.

DESIGN TYPE A2

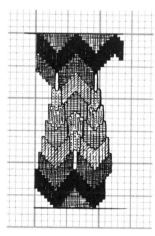

BENCH TOP AND FOOTSTOOL

The bench top could be worked on canvas from the line on p. 27 with the number of stitches in each step altered to give a shallower curve.

The motif can be a version of the shell (A), or any other simplified, compact natural form; a small motif (B) based on an A2 pattern p. 22; or (C), adapted from B2, p. 32; or adapted from part of a grounding.

The motif (C) makes use of coloured background fabric to form the centre of the motif, which if used would be seen against the fabric in the space between the wave lines. If this design were used on canvas, the centre would need to be filled in with counted satin stitch, or with tent stitch surrounding the block shown with a dotted line.

The footstool is worked in wool on canvas, and as with the bench, professionally mounted. The pattern in this particular grounding is deceptive, not being exactly square. It would be advisable to begin in the middle and work outwards.

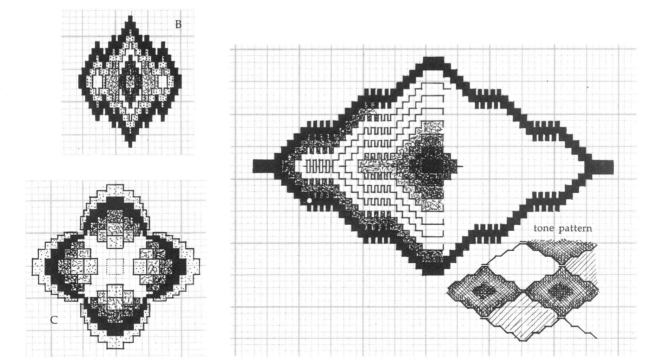

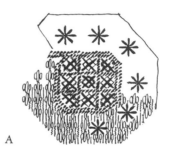

A

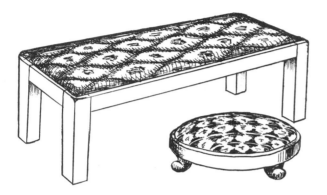

B

C

tone pattern

CUSHIONS

A.

MATERIAL	Pale coffee-coloured coarse Glenshee linen, 18 threads to
THREAD	1″. Stranded cotton (6 strands) and 2 strands of crewel wool.
TO MAKE UP	The design, based on a grounding G7, is enlarged by increasing the number of rows. Motifs are well spaced out to show the background colour.

B.

MATERIAL	Glenshee mercerised cotton fabric, about 19 threads to 1″.
THREAD	A rich cream colour. Stranded cotton (6 strands).
TO MAKE UP	The design, basically the same as that on the hexagonal cushion (p. 68) but with a longer stitch to make sharper points, will need to be drafted on graph paper.

C.

MATERIAL	Yellow Java canvas
THREAD	A heavy wool such as double knitting or Kelim* wool. Anchor soft cotton and 3 strands of crewel wool.
TO MAKE UP	Aida cloth has a distinctive weave which spreads out the embroidery stitches. The scale of this design will depend on thread thickness and on the spacing of rows; there should be at least 7 rows in each band. A fringe of button-hole loops and tassels made of embroidery wool decorates each end. See G7.

D.

MATERIAL	Coloured Glenshee even-weave linen or Willow cross stitch material.
THREAD	1 or 2 strands of crewel wool and a little Sylko Perlé 5 (Pearl cotton).

A widely spaced design which uses a simple grounding motif. G2

*Not available in the United States but used in England and Europe.

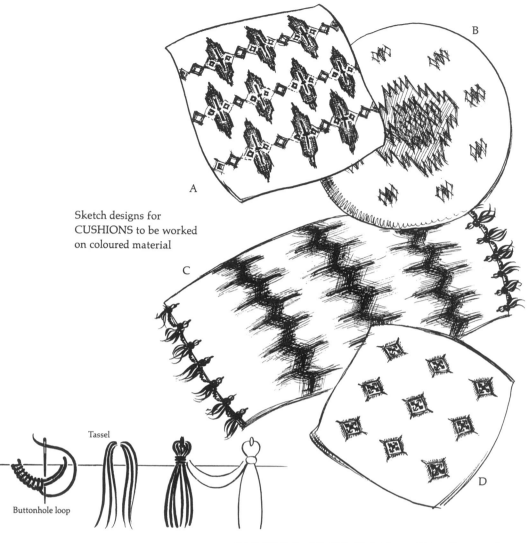

Sketch designs for CUSHIONS to be worked on coloured material

Tassel

Buttonhole loop

HEXAGONAL CUSHION

MATERIAL	Single weave white canvas, 18 threads to 1″ linen for the back. No. 22 tapestry needles
THREAD	3 ply knitting wool
SIZE	14″ x 18″

This design entails accurate counting. Begin with the outline of the central pattern; work those on either side, then the ones between. After this has been done, the design, wholly in 6.3 step, works out easily. Anchor soft or a very

67

thick wool can be introduced to make an unusually heavy line, giving further variation to tone and colour.

TO MAKE UP   Rule pencil lines on the canvas to mark the edge. Trim the canvas to about $\frac{3}{4}''$ from the embroidery and turn under. Turn down the linen straight by the thread and place against the straight thread of the canvas; turn in the diagonal sides with great care not to stretch them out of shape. Tack all round. Oversew on the right side between every wool stitch, at such an angle that the cotton slips between and does not show. Leave one straight edge open until the pad is inserted, then close.

A very fine cord can be added to neaten the edge, but is not essential.

DESIGN TYPE A1

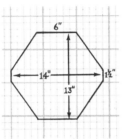

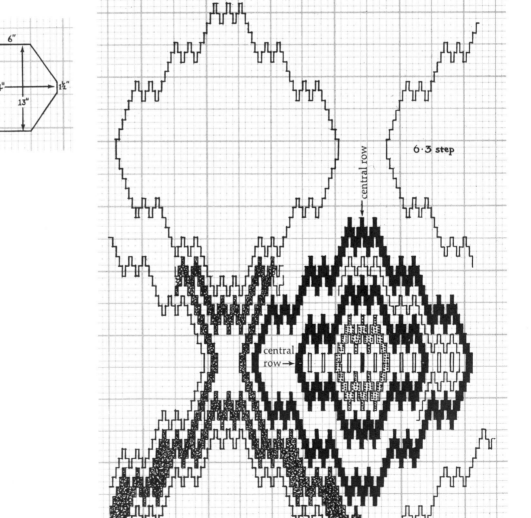

CUSHION

MATERIAL	Hardanger, 22 pairs of threads to 1″, yellow
THREAD	crewel wool
SIZE	13″ square
METHOD	Work begins with the eyelet; the design develops from the first dark zigzag row of Florentine, 4.2 step. Some yellow fabric remains uncovered to form part of the design. Hardanger material appears to be evenly woven; the difference between warp and weft threads is only slight and has little effect on this design. Two threads of crewel wool are used for the motif and one thread for the Hungarian stitch background texture which is worked throughout with the rows in the same direction.

DESIGN TYPE A2

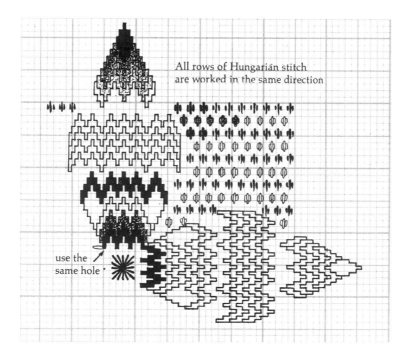

All rows of Hungarian stitch are worked in the same direction

use the same hole

STOOL TOPS

These very simple designs are capable of endless variation. Both can be used in their most obvious form, shading inwards with continuous lines or they can be broken into more elaborate colour arrangements which can be tested on tracing paper laid over the cartoon. Florentine 4.2 step wears better than a longer stitch, but a 6.3 step could be used and further changes made in the number of stitches in the outline. In each diagram the outline is slightly different, showing how easily the design will adapt to fill a given area, such as a stool top which needs re-upholstering.

DESIGN TYPE B2

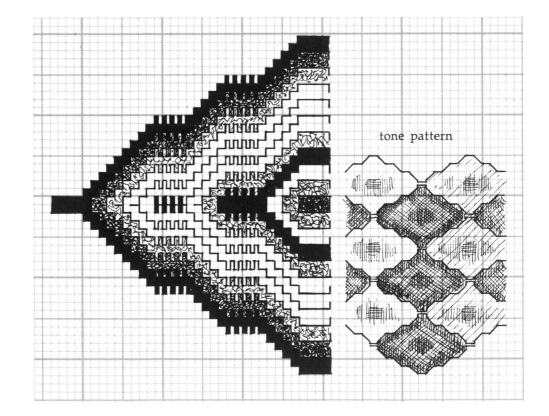

tone pattern

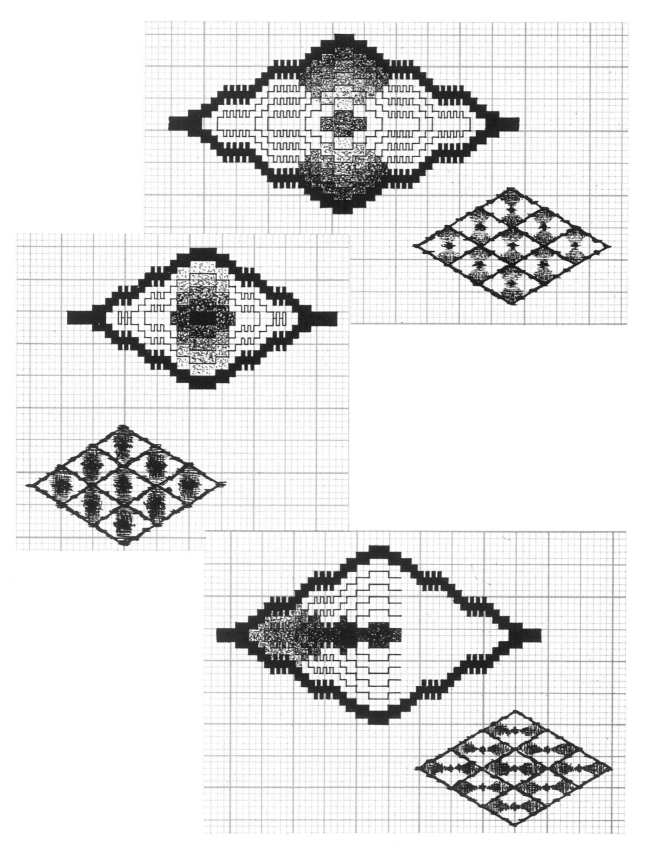

DRESSING STOOL

Both sketches are based on a B I (p. 28) line and are the same except that they are worked with the long edge in the opposite direction. Many shading variations are possible, and provided a limited colour range is chosen, this design will allow fairly strong tone contrasts without becoming garish. An 18 thread to 1″ canvas can be used, with 3 ply knitting wool, tapestry wool or two strands of crewel wool. The work should be mounted professionally.

DESIGN TYPE B1

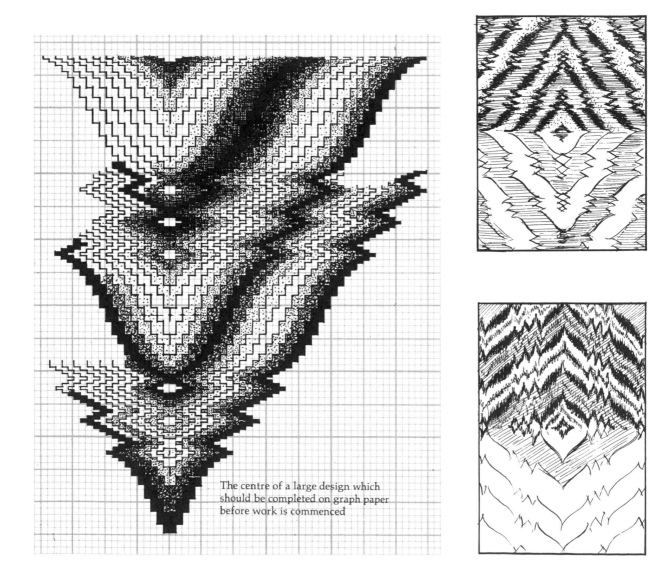

The centre of a large design which should be completed on graph paper before work is commenced

BAGS

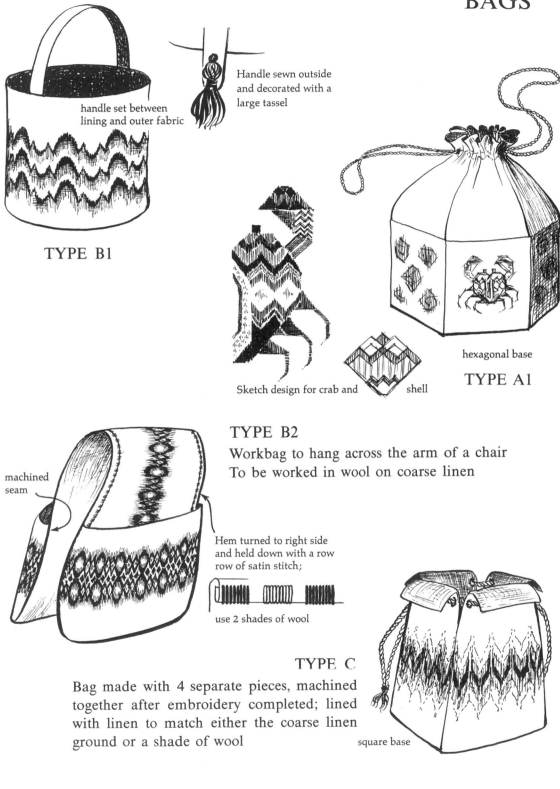

handle set between
lining and outer fabric

Handle sewn outside
and decorated with a
large tassel

TYPE B1

Sketch design for crab and   shell

hexagonal base

TYPE A1

machined
seam

TYPE B2

Workbag to hang across the arm of a chair
To be worked in wool on coarse linen

Hem turned to right side
and held down with a row
row of satin stitch;

use 2 shades of wool

TYPE C

Bag made with 4 separate pieces, machined
together after embroidery completed; lined
with linen to match either the coarse linen
ground or a shade of wool

square base

BAGS TO BE PROFESSIONALLY MOUNTED

All three bags should be worked with crewel wool or stranded cotton, on the finest French canvas available, 24 or preferably 28 threads to 1″, or on Glenshee evenweave linen 28 threads to 1″, if a slightly softer material is preferred. Short stitches are most practical, with an absolute maximum of 8 threads. Designs need to be small and compact, with a frequent enough repeat to build up a satisfactory area of patterned fabric.

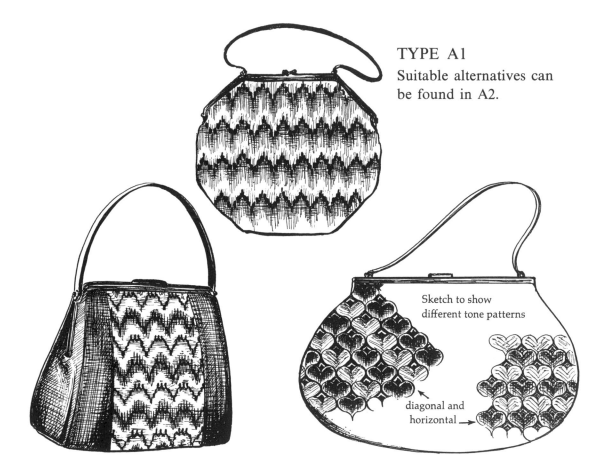

TYPE A1
Suitable alternatives can be found in A2.

Sketch to show different tone patterns

diagonal and horizontal

TYPE E3
Worked in Hungarian point

TYPE B2
With the motif reversed

SCUFFS

MATERIAL	Single thread white canvas, 23 threads to 1″ Wadding for extra softness over slipper soles Cotton lining. Bias binding
THREAD	Crewel wool, dark and mid brown, fawn, blue and pale pink
TO MAKE UP	Sew the bias binding all round the under edge of the sole; pad the upper surface and tack the lining in place leaving a space on either side of the tread for the embroidered band to be inserted. Line the band, pin in position and if possible, test across the foot to ensure a firm grip. When the band is in place between lining and sole, secure one side, then fasten the other which is far less easy to do, (a long darning needle helps to negotiate an awkward piece of sewing). Finally bring the binding level with the top edge of the sole and oversew all round with very small stitches.

DESIGN TYPE B2

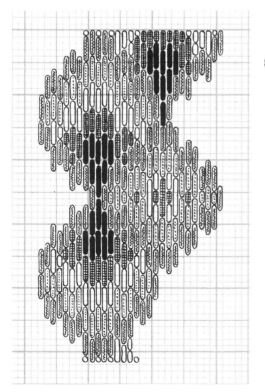

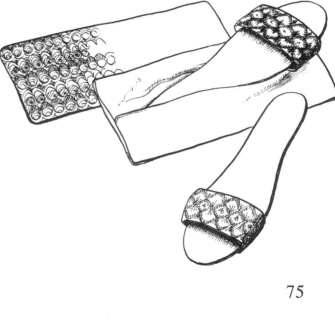

SLIPPER OR GLOVE CASE

MATERIAL	Single thread white canvas, 23 threads to 1″ or Glenshee embroidery fabric 18 threads to 1″, a firm but softer material than canvas
	Brown corded cotton lining
THREAD	Crewel wool, shades of yellow, blue, blue-green, greyish-brown, grey
SIZE	4¼″ x 10¾″
TO MAKE UP	Trim the canvas to within about ¼″ of the embroidery, turn under and catch back. Oversew the embroidered panel on to the lining. Neaten both long edges; overlap as if making a pillow case, and machine the two short seams.

DESIGN TYPE B2

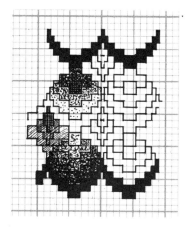

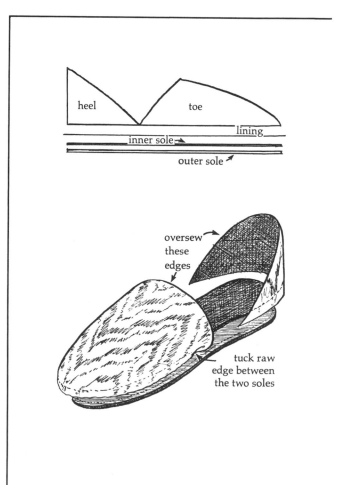

76

SLIPPERS

MATERIAL	Single thread canvas, 20 threads to 1″
	Stiffening, wadding, cotton lining, soles
THREAD	Crewel wool
TO MAKE UP	Pad, stiffen and line the heel piece, oversewing the curved seam from the right side; leave the lower edge free. Pad the toe piece. Oversew from the right side the curved instep edge, leaving the long curve tacked. Heel and toe must be attached between the bottom of the sole and its lining. On a lamb's-wool sole the edge can be prized up and the slipper pieces eased underneath, tacked, then sewn firmly in place. If separate soles are used, line the inner sole, paste down the edges of the lining to the sole and pin to the outer sole at the instep before sewing heel and toe in place.

DESIGN TYPE E4

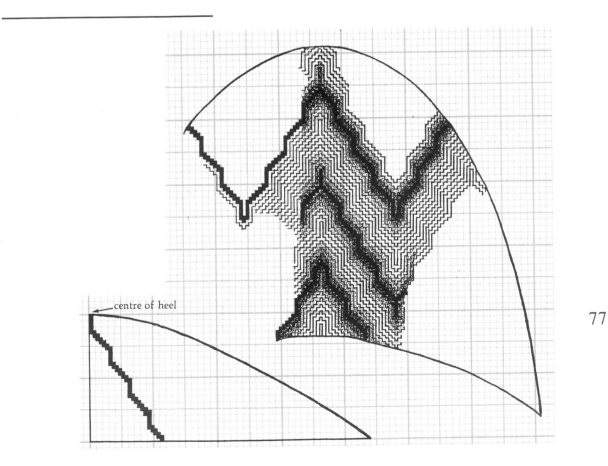

centre of heel

77

GLASSES' CASE

MATERIAL	Single thread canvas, 23 threads to 1″
	Stiffening; either linen or corded silk lining
THREAD	Stranded cotton
SIZE	About 3″ x 6½″
TO MAKE UP	Cover two pieces of stiffening material with the lining by pasting down the edges. Place right sides together and oversew all round except for the opening. Turn down the canvas edges. Place wrong sides together and oversew with large shallow "tacks" to hold the two sides lightly in place. Slip the lining inside. Use a paper knife to slip along inside to make certain that the canvas turning lies flat. Tack the open end to prevent the lining from sliding out. Oversew the two pieces of canvas together, between every embroidery stitch. It is much easier to insert the lining before the canvas is tightly sewn. Finally close both seams at the open end.

GROUNDINGS are most suitable

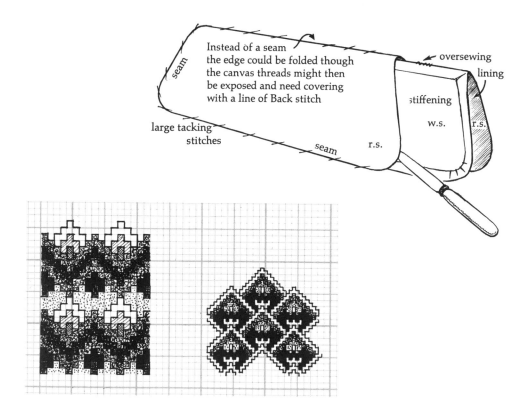

78

STOOL TOP

MATERIAL   Aida canvas, green fabric only partly covered with embroidery
THREAD   Tapestry wool in shades of green and grey

A complete cartoon need not be drawn; a sketch gives suffi-cient guidance and allows for ideas to evolve from the stitches as work progresses. Very little counting is needed when the pattern keeps to the same step, Florentine 4.2, and a few other stitches such as Hungarian and star stitch. This diagram shows that unless tones are carefully considered an abstract design can quickly become dis-jointed. Those areas of material not covered by stitches must balance one another.

STOLE

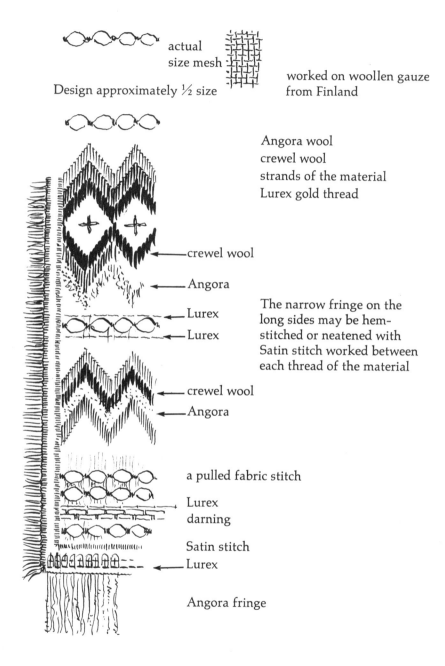

actual
size mesh

worked on woollen gauze
from Finland

Design approximately ½ size

Angora wool
crewel wool
strands of the material
Lurex gold thread

crewel wool

Angora

The narrow fringe on the
long sides may be hem-
stitched or neatened with
Satin stitch worked between
each thread of the material

Lurex

Lurex

crewel wool

Angora

a pulled fabric stitch

Lurex
darning

Satin stitch

Lurex

Angora fringe

80

If fine flannel, red,
white, pale grey or
natural, with a
fairly loose weave
is substituted for the
woollen gauze, drawn
thread work must take
the place of pulled
fabric work

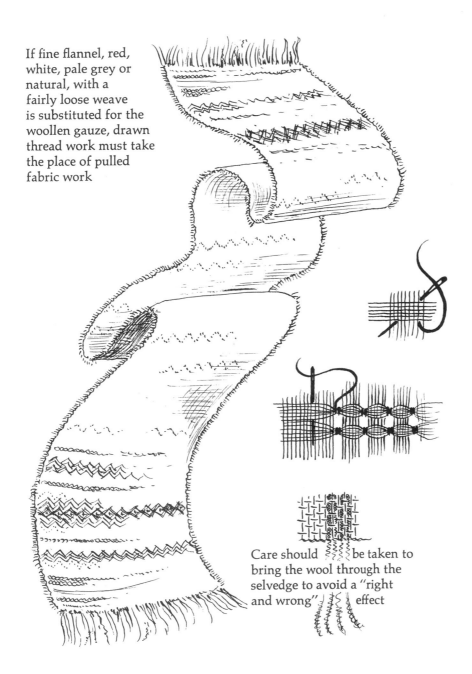

Care should be taken to
bring the wool through the
selvedge to avoid a "right
and wrong" effect

VANITY BAG

MATERIAL	Willow cross stitch fabric, grey
	Linen lining, green
	Transparent plastic sheeting
	6″ zip fastener. Pearl and bronze beads
THREAD	Stranded cotton, stone, grey, lime green, white
	Sylko perlé, No 5 (Pearl cotton), stone
SIZE	6½″ x 4¼″
TO MAKE UP	Tack a guide line to indicate finished size. Do not cut the material to shape until the embroidery is finished. The first complete line of stitches is worked far enough from the top edge to allow room for the adjusted line (see diag.) to be added when the rest of the embroidery is finished. Several rows at the bottom also need adjustment at each end, to fit to the curve of the bag. When completed, place face downwards on a soft surface, press, ironing outwards from the centre. Do not damp. Sew on the beads. Cut the fabric to shape, tack the side seams straight by the thread and machine them. Machine green linen and plastic lining together, making them very slightly smaller to fit inside the bag. One edge of the zip can be machined between lining and outer fabric, the other edge must be finished by hand. Great care must be taken to set the zip in straight. Make a small tassel from embroidery thread to finish the zip tag.

DESIGN TYPE C

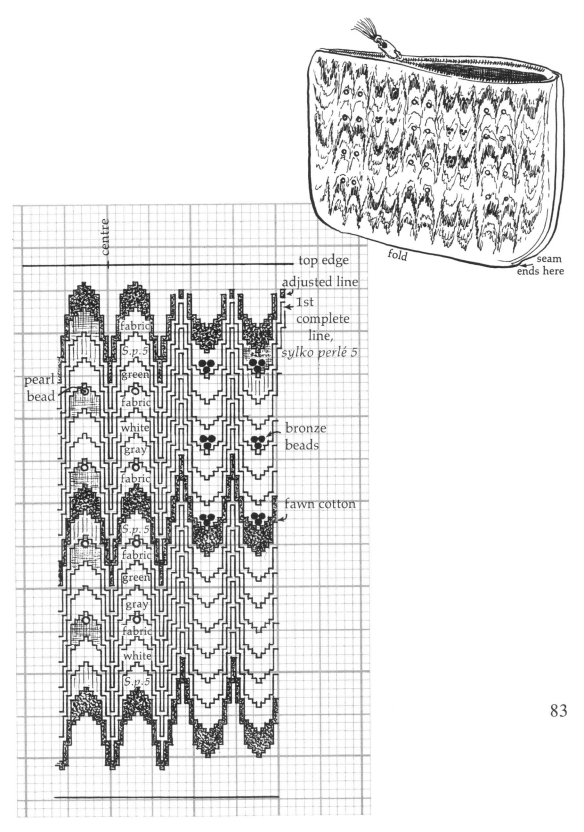

fold

seam ends here

centre

top edge

adjusted line

1st complete line, *sylko perlé 5*

fabric

S.p. 5

green

fabric

pearl bead

white

gray

fabric

bronze beads

fawn cotton

S.p. 5

fabric

green

gray

fabric

white

S.p. 5

83

CHILD'S APRON

MATERIAL	Willow even-weave, white
THREAD	Stranded cotton, pink, cerise, blue, green
	4 strands used for embroidery
	Hemstitching worked with one strand of the fabric
TO MAKE UP	To prevent fraying while work is in progress, turn under and tack hems at a distance from the final edge. When the embroidery is finished, count threads on either side and see that each hem has the same number of threads when turned under. On coarse material even one extra thread makes a noticeable difference to the width. Turn up the bottom hem straight by the thread. Cut away a small piece at each end to make the corners lie flat. Remove one thread and work handkerchief hemstitch. Embroider the band with satin stitch and star stitches; make up the ties, hemming into each thread of the fabric. This method is easier than turning inside out when the band is narrow or the fabric frays. Having made small pleats at the top of the apron, set it into the band, tacking into place by the thread to keep it straight and finally hemming along the back.

DESIGN TYPE B1

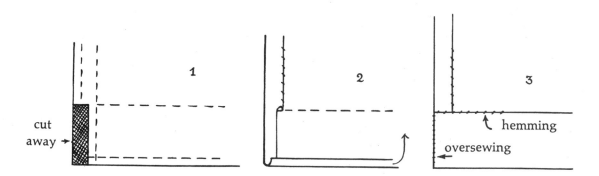

How to turn a corner with different width hems

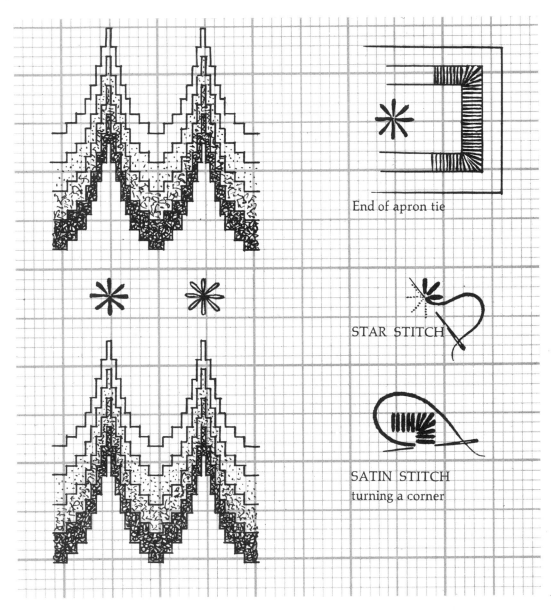

End of apron tie

STAR STITCH

SATIN STITCH
turning a corner

See page 18 for picture of apron.

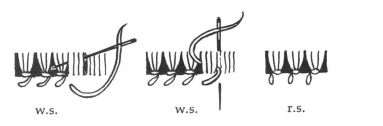

w.s.   w.s.   r.s.

Hem stitch

85

BELL PULL AND TIE BACK
FOR DRAPERY

To be worked in wool or stranded cotton and a little Sylko
Perlé on canvas

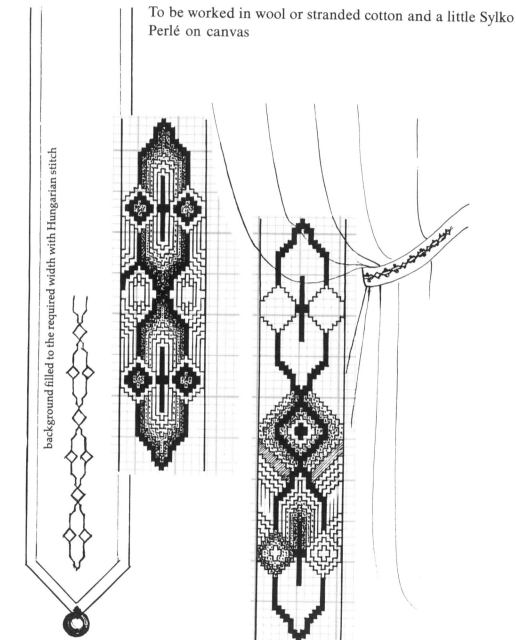

background filled to the required width with Hungarian stitch

86

DECORATIVE PANELS

To be worked on coloured even-weave material in various
threads, or on red flannel in different thicknesses of white
thread and a little very dark red

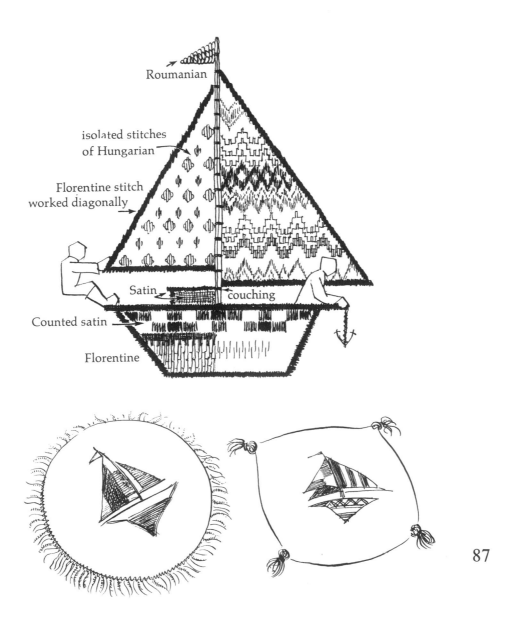

Roumanian

isolated stitches
of Hungarian

Florentine stitch
worked diagonally

Satin

couching

Counted satin

Florentine

FLORENTINE EMBROIDERY

DECORATIVE PANELS · SHIPS

A series of small panels to hang beside a child's bed

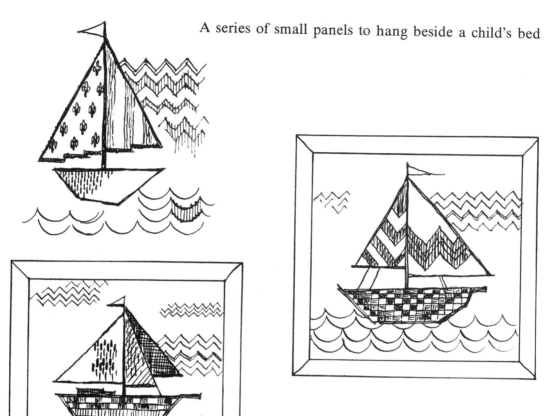

DECORATIVE PANELS · SHIPS

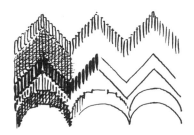

Patterns used to cover
the background.
Diagrams to show the transition

from zigzag to curve

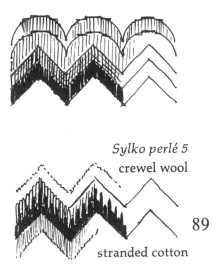

Sylko perlé 5
crewel wool

89

stranded cotton

DECORATIVE PANEL · FISH

Design development,
first sketch and
stitch suggestions
(AUTHOR'S COPYRIGHT)

When the panel was embroidered
a mistake in the number of stitches,
4 being used instead of 3, led to difficulty throughout the work.

Hungarian

Brick

Sketch for a panel or cushion
to be worked on even-weave
linen, royal blue or jade,
25 threads to 1″

DECORATIVE PANELS · OWL

Embroidered on Norland openweave linen in crewel wool, stranded cotton and threads of the material itself. Lines of pulled fabric work make a light background texture. The loose weave of the fabric helped to create the pattern on the breast. The wings in Florentine stitch 6.2 step are worked in diagonal rows, a speedy method used on some Italian 17th century bedcovers. (AUTHOR'S COPYRIGHT)

Student's sketch in strong black outline and water-colour. Curves became straight lines when translated into stitches.

pulled fabric

Eventual alteration in wing shape has not improved upon the original idea.

DECORATIVE PANEL · ROOSTER

Design notes from a student's sketch book

DECORATIVE PANEL · BISON

Prehistoric painting which inspired a design on canvas

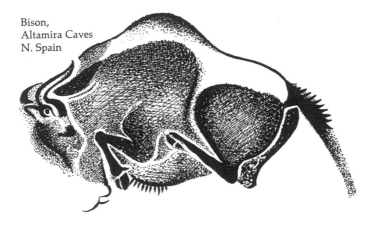

Bison,
Altamira Caves
N. Spain

A student's interpretation of a similar Altamira bison; the work was carried out mainly in shades of bronze, golden brown, olive green and grey.

Framed panel

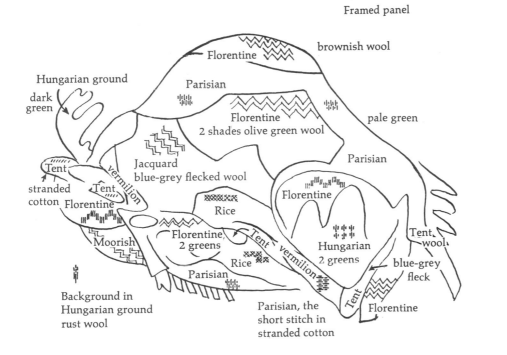

93

SUNFLOWER

Sunflower, 10″ x 9″, worked in shades of lime green, greenish yellow, gold, orange and red crewel wool on lemon yellow linen scrim, embellished with pearl dewdrops and viridian, green, bronze, gunmetal and jet faceted beads (AUTHOR'S COPYRIGHT)

THE PLACE OF FLORENTINE EMBROIDERY IN ECCLESIASTICAL WORK

Ecclesiastical work is a specialised branch of embroidery, in which Florentine stitch and Hungarian point can have only a limited use because, on the whole, the patterns produced tend to be dominating. If, however, they are chosen with discretion, having due regard for suitability of scale and colour, more handsome work could be done today than in 17th century Italy when numerous vestments and altar frontals were made. Florentine embroidery has proved its adaptability and could with care combine with symbolic designs and the traditional colours of the church to decorate the following articles:—

Alms or collecting bags
Altar frontals
Banners (if used among other stitches)
Communion rail kneelers
Cushions, (as a book rest or missal stand for pulpit or altar)
Door curtains
Kneeling pads (without gusset)
Kneelers or hassocks (with gusset)
Lectern falls
Sanctuary hassocks (usually several inches deeper than kneelers)

Index